Overcoming Sadness, Sorrow, Despair and Hopelessness

By Blake Walker

ISBN-13: 978-1492259046
ISBN-10: 1492259047

Overcoming Sadness, Sorrow, Despair and Hopelessness

CONTENTS

INTRODUCTION

Almost everyone at one time or another in their life has experienced some degree of sadness from being a compassionate witness or victim of life's occasional harsh consequences. Eventually, deaths of parents, siblings, relatives, and close friends bring home the heavy burdens of deep sorrow. At times, it seems no matter what we try to do, how hard we try and even after throwing in all of our life's resources, we still fail to bring about a positive outcome and begin to slip into despair. The feeling of hopelessness from profound despair cannot be explained unless one has been in that awful lonely place that settles in the pit of one's solar plexus, at what might be the focus of one's soul.

Unfortunately, some people never make it back and some have taken the easy way out to deaden the pain through alcoholism, drug addiction… and ultimately suicide. Never in my life had I allowed a feeling of loneliness and depression last so long as after I had to give up all of my bunnies for adoption because I could not afford to give them a good life anymore due to financial reversals. When I was a college freshman, my first girlfriend was told by her parents to drop me or they'd drop her out of UCSB. It was my fault for spending the night with her in her all women's dormitory. I was depressed, couldn't eat and cried everyday for a month. I felt like I was dying, and thought of ways to end that terrible feeling.

It appears that these emotions develop in a linear progression, as sadness is not resolved, it slips into sorrow. As sorrow deepens, it transforms into despair. When despair knows no bounds... one's life becomes hopeless. And finally, in seeking to escape hopelessness, addictions leading to death occur. Some people cling to religion for a spiritual uplift from the destructive path of hopelessness. Others become involved in causes greater than themselves to take the focus away from their own frailties by serving those more unfortunate. Still, emotional support from loved ones or focusing on constructive or recreational activities relieves the depression of despair and hopelessness. For most people who have felt some degree of sadness, sorrow and despair, they have been able to maintain sufficient happiness and contentment in various aspects of their lives to keep from falling into the pit of hopelessness. For some, the emotional well is just too deep to climb out of, even with a safety line thrown in by others who seek to help.

We hear of lovers who become heartbroken, and parents who lose their only child. We feel sympathy for those who lose everything through a wildfire or other natural disaster beyond their ability to either prevent or survive. And we are ashamed to truly attempt to understand homelessness and abject poverty. Yet, most people set upon themselves the task of rebuilding their lives and souls after tragedies because the other option is too frightening to fathom. No one wants to slip into darkness to vanish into anonymity and hopeless despair, but unfortunately, there are plenty of individuals who eventually succumb to it.

This book attempts to discuss the path to self-destruction, whether it is internally or externally precipitated as a reaction to hurtful and painful events and circumstances in life. We examine the lives of various individuals, and how their final despair resulted in death, and the effect of their loss to those who loved them. No one is an island unto oneself, and as life events often trigger despair, those who suffer the loss of loved ones then become drawn in to the cycle of sadness, sorrow, despair and hopelessness. What are some of the solutions to prevent the ultimate suffering and sacrifice of life from the well of hopelessness? If perhaps some of the answers suggested herein will help to save even one person, then the effort in writing this book has been well worthwhile.

CHAPTER 1 – What makes people happy, content and hopeful in life?

In order to understand what makes people sad, depressed, miserable and hopeless, we need first to examine what makes most people happy. Certainly in most part, happiness is the opposite of unhappiness as much as being financially secured is the opposite of poverty. Happy people are rarely if ever sad, miserable and hopeless. People with generally content and happy lives exhibit certain universal commonalities, including:

- Fulfilling relationships and successful careers
- Acceptance and feeling loved by significant partner
- Financial stability and security
- Excellent energetic good health free of illnesses or injuries
- Shared meaningful and enjoyable experiences with loved ones
- Sufficient ownership and enjoyment of material possessions and comforts
- Many options and alternatives on a daily basis to enjoy others and life
- Freedom from excruciating physical pain and suffering
- No issues that cause emotional pain and suffering
- Secure and comfortable home in safe neighborhood
- Emotional gratification and validation

- Few if any unresolved major problems
- A feeling of realistic individual empowerment
- Little or no fear or anxiety of future events
- Satisfied realistic social expectations
- Treated fairly in all aspects of life
- No hiding secrets of wrong doings in the closet
- No worry of discovery for wrong doings, secret lives or sexual preferences
- High freedom of pursuing and expressing personal independence
- Moral consistency that fulfills religious or spiritual ideals
- No legal or government persecution or prosecution
- Progressive attainment of dreams and goals
- Positive hopeful worldview and philosophical perspectives

When people are lacking in any combination of these "happiness factors", they could lose a sense of self-esteem and conclude that their lives have no value to anyone, not even to themselves. These types of thoughts when persistent, become etched into one's consciousness and subconscious when then restlessly dream about such scenarios. The solution and prevention of depression that isn't bio-chemically caused, is simple... "Don't worry, be happy!" But that is easy to say, but to most people, not easy to accomplish. To some, it seems impossible.

Chapter 2 - His story - Dale, forever positive and happy?

Let's describe what a highly content, happy and fulfilled person could look like in the following example of real people who have attained this temporary or sustained immunity to sadness, sorrow, despair and hopelessness. We will name this illustrative but representational person as Dale (either sex or gender):

Dale is in an understanding, sharing, caring, loving and fulfilling committed relationship with no desire to wander or seek additional affairs. As a mid-level professional careerist, Dale is respected and admired for competent expertise by peers and bosses, with regular recognition on a fast promotional track in a highly successful career. Dale receives an abundance of acceptance and the feeling of being loved unconditionally by the significant partner, who partakes in an equal effort to bring about their immediate financial stability and long-term security.

Dale and his partner enjoy excellent daily energetic good health that has been free of illnesses or injuries, and consequently focuses on their shared meaningful and enjoyable experiences with each other and those they love who love them back. Both Dale and his partner have achieved sufficient ownership and enjoyment of material possessions and comforts and find many options and alternatives on a daily basis to enjoy others and their lives together or occasionally apart resulting from mutual respect, honesty and trust. They have freedom from excruciating pain and suffering, whether physical or emotional and both feel a peaceful contentment that reflects their emotional balance.

They live in a secure and comfortable home in safe neighborhood, surrounded by friendly neighbors who demonstrate high levels of goodwill. Their lives are emotional gratifying and they feel validated through their achievements and blessed by their good fortune to have a loving family and wonderful friends, all of whom have few if any unresolved major problems, as is with their situation. A feeling of realistic individual empowerment with little or no fear or anxiety of future events envelops their beings that are reinforced by their high degree of social satisfaction due to their routine attainment of realistic social expectations.

Both feel they are have been and are treated fairly in all aspects of their lives and neither are hiding secrets of wrong doings in their emotional closets because they are upfront and honest people who never harm others. Consequently, neither have any worries of discovery for wrong doings, secret lives or unexpressed sexual preferences. As a result of this emotional openness, both appreciated a high level of freedom to pursue and express their personal independence and mobility, either as a shared team effort or separately without any hesitation or concern the other might become envious, jealous or hurt.

One of the guiding lights in their daily lives is the moral consistency that fulfills their religious and spiritual ideals that prohibits them from wrong doings, and consequently, they never have to fear legal or government persecution or prosecution. Instead, both work daily toward reaching their progressive attainment of shared and independent dreams and goals and consequently have developed a very positive and hopeful worldview in their philosophical perspectives of personal responsibility with charity for the less fortunate. They answer anyone who ask if they are happy with an emphatic YES, but it's rare to be asked this question as their happy smiles, fulfilling lives, and wonderful family and social circumstances make them exude happiness for all to see in the light of day that illuminates the darkest hours experienced by others.

Psychologists, medical and genetic researchers have tried to determine what causes some people to fall into severe irrecoverable depression leading to suicide, versus those who are able to climb out from the emotional abyss. There appears to be seems to be some genetic components to happiness, some attitudinal (it's mind over matter... what you don't mind won't matter), some learned cultural mindset, and some unknowns as to why there are people who suffer horrendous personal losses, but still continue to be positive and happy. If we could figure out what makes people happy, then certainly the opposite components are what make people sad, right?

Chapter 3 - Why people become sad and hopeless

Wouldn't it feel great to be happy and fulfilled in all areas of our lives? Certainly, but there are probably more people who are lonely, unhappy, unfulfilled, miserable, sad, dejected and hopeless than those who have been lucky enough or worked hard enough to attain content and balanced lives. In most case, people are burdened in their lives with various unresolved conflicts and issues that impact their mental, physical, emotional, social and economic health. Let's look as some of the issues that are obstacles to attaining happiness but instead become the anchors to people's discontent.

What causes sadness, sorrow, despair and hopelessness? Here's a list of arguable the top two dozen causes of unhappiness and misery:

- Failure in relationships, career
- Rejection and/or replacement by significant partner
- Financial ruination
- Debilitating Illnesses or injuries
- Loss of loved ones
- Catastrophic material losses
- No practical or conceivable way out of misery

- Long term excruciating physical pain and suffering
- Emotional pain and suffering
- Loneliness leading to despondency
- Sudden poverty and/or homelessness
- Profound emotional disappointments
- Cumulative unresolved major problems
- Total helplessness, real or perceived
- Fear induced severe anxiety of future
- Unattainable Social expectations
- Injustice without relief
- Keeping long term secrets of wrong doings
- Sustained fear of discovery for wrong doings
- Lost of personal independence
- Moral hypocrisy causing sustained cognitive dissonance
- Legal or government persecution and/or prosecution
- Unfulfilled dreams and goals
- Negative worldview and philosophical perspectives

Unlike the story of Dale, whose apparent happiness is his "normal" state, the question we must answer is what makes some people succumb to a profound feeling of overwhelming depression to the point of despair and hopelessness? At what point do severely depressed people make that horrible decision to end their own lives because they can no longer bear the deep emotional pain? What are they lacking in their lives that they cannot recover from catastrophic personal losses, whether based on relationships, financial reversals, medical pain and suffering, or bio-chemical reactions. One thing seems sure, so-called "normal" people, with healthy lives are not immune to sudden onsets of depression. The on set of despair doesn't necessarily indicate a persistent state of sadness or depression, but rather there are triggers that can result from one incident, or a series or accumulation of events that in the aggregate result in emotional slippage down the slippery slope of hopelessness.

Chapter 4 - Her story – Jaime, a cascade of catastrophic losses

Let's take a closer look at an example of Jaime who has experienced a string of failure in relationships after his career tanked after being laid off during the 2009 recession. Following his financial collapse, his partner was also laid off from work. This causes much consternation and stress in their relationship, and once they became broke, Jaime was rejected and replaced by another person who was gainfully employed and lived in a large house.

The stress from financial ruination contributed to a debilitating Illness, and Jaime had succumbed to a broken elbow resulting from falling out of bed while ill.

On top of this misfortunes and misery, Jaime's elderly parents were both killed in a wildfire. The loss of both loved ones was heart wrenchingly painful, but as the parent's primary caregiver, Jaime also suffered catastrophic material losses of everything, including his parent's new home he lived in for a decade. Due to the recession, the value of his parent's house plummeted and was technically "upside down" so the insurance company settled with the lender, and Jaime became homeless except for the clothes worn on the day of the fire, and the car that was at work at that time. Jaime just didn't see a realistic way out of misery.

After six months turned into a long term excruciating emotional pain and suffering, his physical pain and suffering from his injury seemed to be magnified and regaining the full use of the broken elbow came with much pain. Jaime's sudden poverty and homelessness was a profound emotional disappointment that only added to his already full plate of cumulative unresolved major problems. Jaime began to feel totally helplessness and didn't know where to start looking for help, or even who might be willing to help. It seems all friends and family just vanished from the face of the Earth. This fear of an uncertain future induced severe anxiety. Murphy's Law... what's the next bad thing waiting to happen? When will the next shoe fall?

Jaime had been modestly successful at maintaining social relations, but now with everyone he knew becoming elusive, social expectations became daunting and unsatisfied. It appeared no one wants to know a broke derelict living out of an old car. If there is a God, then Jaime felt that his situation was an injustice without relief and mercy from a supposedly loving, kind and powerful God. Jaime had too much time to think, and all the secrets of wrong doings that were festering kept wanting to surface and a severe anxiety developed from the fear of discovery. Jaime didn't want to admit anything for fear of losing personal independence, even though a profound feeling of moral hypocrisy caused sustained cognitive dissonance that was uncomfortable to say the least. Fear of legal or government persecution or prosecution for various hidden past crimes caused recurring nightmares. Instead of focusing on unfulfilled dreams and goals, Jaime developed a defensive negative worldview and philosophical perspective where society created another victim and consequently, any future actions or behaviors with negative consequences would be blamed on society.

For about a year, I was a funeral escort motorcycle rider who attended many funerals after the funeral processions. After we accomplished the sometimes tricky and always dangerous process of escorting funeral participants in their vehicles safely to their funerals, death was waiting the relatives and friends of those deceased. Mourners often broke down in tears, and I especially remembered the children of fallen parents who sobbed, sometimes uncontrollably and had to be comforted by adults in attendance. I will never forget some of those moments of grief and despair.

Of course, as a macho motorcycle rider among a team who routinely exposed themselves to the dangers of the road, I eventually became the only rider left who wasn't involved in a vehicle accident during our escorting duties. I witnessed a vehicle plow into a partner's motorcycle when attempting to bolt through a green light that was being halted for the funeral procession. Another time, a truck tried to split the space between procession vehicles, and cause a major wreck. The danger of death was ever present.

Chapter 5 - THEIR STORIES – The suffering and deaths I've witnessed

Have you ever experienced a person actually dying while in your arms? How about over a dozen times?   How easy is that?   Not easy for one, or over a dozen. Sadness, sorrow, despair and hopelessness can envelope one's soul. Let's take a brief glimpse at some heart wrenching stories that happen everyday to people all around the world, and the dire emotional challenges that they face in attempting to overcome the inevitable deaths of loved ones. It is almost certain that everyone living will eventually suffer the grief from the deaths of their parents or close friends and relatives.

The stories that follow happen to families everyday, wide and far from every walk of life. Their stories are unique, but not uncommon. People are born without a choice, and short of intentional suicide, one day down the road die without a choice. In between, people's lives tend to be filled with challenges, disappointments, hurt, suffering, and many times, abuse, neglect, and other tragedies. Occasionally, people find ways to escape their problems for moments through alcohol, drugs, or sexual encounters… only to have to pay dearly for those times down the road. A few remarkable souls find happiness in spite of it.

If your story is worse than these, please share it with the world through You Tube, Face Book or Twitter, because we want to know. When you get responses, ignore the haters and focus on those who wish you well and really care because your stories have touched their hearts and souls.

- Father Dearest – My DAD…

My 86-year-old father was out for his daily senior citizen hourly walk around the neighborhood along with my then 78-year-old mother. It was a terribly hot day, and neither took along drinking water because they never did and always made it back before the hour was up. But not on that particular day. My dad decided to take an unscheduled detour to see more of the neighborhood and they became lost as he was not aware of the street signs and neither of them being elderly recalled which way they turned. Instead of knocking on a stranger's door and asking for directions, my stubborn macho father refused to listen to my mother's suggestion to do so, and they pressed on. Half an hour passed, then another half hour.

They both became exhausted, but my aged father became dehydrated and fainted on the sidewalk, fortunately he didn't fall down headfirst but as he got faint, he fell to his knee with his arms holding him up. My mother helped him down to the sidewalk and she plead to a woman who was watering her lawn a few houses down for help. Fortunately, the woman was a retired nurse and recognized the situation.

She gave my dad some water and slowly he sat up on the curb. When he seemed a bit more functional, she and my tiny mother helped him up into her car and this kind lady drove my parents home.

I was staying with my elderly parents during the evenings after work during the week and my sisters each helped out during the weekend so I could return to my own place to have a break. After work when I got to my parent's house, mom mother told me my dad had earlier in the day fallen down and couldn't get up. I talked to my dad and he seemed okay and was resting in bed. A few days later, I got a call at work that my dad had fallen backwards down the three steps at our front porch, so I rushed home. Worried he had stuck his head, I asked him where he struck the paved walkway and examined him. He said as he lost his balance, he fell backwards when attempting to step up, and struck his back on the steps, but his head hit the thick grass of the front lawn, just missing the metal sprinkler head.

I rushed him to Kaiser Permanente's Urgent Care Center in Baldwin Park and let the Triage Nurse know he had passed out a couple days earlier from exhaustion and dehydration, and had just fallen down bruising his back and shoulder, and may have had a concussion. As usual, the room was filled with people of a wide range of ages complaining of a various assortment of ailments from twisted ankles to stomach aches. I informed the staff that my elderly

Dad had a history of heart problems. They took his blood pressure reading and it was 240/160. I asked the nurse if that seemed extremely high, and she said she would write it in his chart and the doctor would determine what to do next.

I took my dad there through rush hour traffic by 6:00 PM, and the staff did nothing but make us sit and wait. I requested they should give him some pain medication for his back injury and they said he would have to wait for the doctor's evaluation. Hours went by, evening turned to night... night became day. I asked staff on many occasions to see my dad, and they declined. Finally, at 5AM, I called my eldest sister to inform her that I had to go home to get ready for another day of work, without any sleep the night before. She met me at Kaiser (she was a department manager at another location, so she had some flex time) by 6AM and I explained how the Kaiser staff had done absolutely nothing for our father who had a 240/160 BP. She said she would take care of it.

I called my sister as I was leaving for work at 7AM and she informed me our father was being examined... more than 12 hours later at an urgent care facility! I felt that was unacceptable, but didn't protest to Kaiser Administration for fear of retribution against my sister. Later that evening after work, I returned to my parent's home and my dad was resting and taking medication for his pain and his regular blood pressure medication. My sister told me he didn't have any broken bones and it didn't seem he had a concussion, and the doctor said he should be fine with some rest, but to make sure he stays hydrated and not walk when the temperature is too hot outside. Good advice.

A week later, this time on the weekend, my father fell again. Fortunately he was on the front lawn picking up his newspaper when it happened. My mom called and I rushed over to help him up from the lawn, as my mother wasn't strong enough to help, and none of the neighbors either noticed or wanted to get involved. I purposefully lived about a ten minutes drive from my parents, so by the time I got there, my mom was still attending my dad and had his head on a pillow on the grass. I helped him up… and he felt stiff and heavy, as he wasn't cooperating very much. He had trouble lifting his feet so it was a bit of a struggle to walk him up, with his arm around my shoulder and my arms around his waist.

I got him into bed, and told my eldest sister about the incident. We agreed to make an appointment with his regular family doctor so he could get examined along with blood work, an EEG and EKG. When the results were in a week later, it appeared my father had a mini-stroke. We couldn't determine if it was from his dehydration during his ill fated walk on a horribly hot day when he fainted, or did his 12 hour wait for assistance at Kaiser's Urgent Care contribute to his condition that might have been treated more expeditiously to prevent further damage. We will never know. I suspected they had an intern on staff and they perhaps hoped my father would have a heart attack so they could give the intern some experience treating a heart-attack patient. When I was waiting there all night long with my father, no one that night came in with a heart attack, so I suppose it's on the intern's medical school requirement to have treated a heart attack. It may sound despicable and sinister, but one of my nephews was a medical student, and he had a checklist of conditions that he needed to be trained on before he could graduate. The medical profession is shrouded in mystery.

A month later, my father could no longer walk on his own. I got a wheel chair for him and he became bedridden except when I was there to help him up and down from bed into the wheel chair to take him to dinner in the dining room and for all subsequent family celebrations for the next two years. We hired a home health care assistant to help my mother with my dad while I was at work, and I helped monitor and service my dad during the evenings and night so my mother could get her sleep in. My dad needed his adult diapers to be changed nightly and needed water and snacks whenever he woke, so that was my job. Since the period of 2006 to 2009, I rarely got a full night's sleep, except on the weekends when I would sometimes binge drink and it knocked me out good.

Sometimes, the lack of restful sleep made me less efficient at work, but I don't think anyone really ever noticed. Since that time, I grew into the habit of getting up at least once during the night, while I used to sleep through the night. I don't know if that's a habit I formed, or it might just be part of my aging process. At any rate, my sister suggested we should place him on the Hospice program and to complete an advanced medical directive. As my sister was a Kaiser employee and familiar with their health care perspectives and treatment options, we signed on. My dad's condition was stable, but was slowly deteriorating due to the aging process. It appeared he was developing a mild case of Parkinson Disease as his hands would tremble slightly at the beginning and six months later he was unable to grasp. He was also losing his hearing and awareness. He was diagnosed as having Dementia. He was slowly slipping away.

Around two and half years after his initial fall, and six months after he was enrolled in the Hospice program, he passed away during the early morning around 4AM, but no one knew he had died. My mother said when she checked on him, he has his hand in his mouth and she didn't think anything of that. When she rose to help with his morning routine before the health care worker arrived, she found he was not breathing and had turned pale around 7AM. I had spent that night at my own home with my girlfriend because my second sister was staying the night to give me a break to catch up on my sleep. No sooner had I sat down at my workstation and powered up my computer when I received a call at 8:30AM from my sister that my father had passed away.

I started to tear up, and told my supervisor, a very compassionate person who advised me to go home right away and we'd figure out my workload and attendances report later when I got back... four days later. When I got home, my mother and sister had been crying, but I stayed strong so they wouldn't have to freak out, and within an hour the Hearst from the funeral home arrived. They removed my father's body on a gurney and placed him into the Hearst, as my mother waited by the front door. My sister and I thanked the transporters from the funeral home, and we confirmed that we had not called 911 or requested emergency services since my father was already dead. As they drove off, my mother broke down into hysterical sobbing and my sister said goodbye very loudly to my departing dad's body. While we had all expected he would be passing, it was still surreal and seemed like a scene from a movie. I was watching myself as in an out of body experience, similar to my witnessing other families grieve when I was a funeral escort motorcycle rider during my younger days. It was very sad. There was nothing more we could do.

Now my task was to watch over my mother to make sure she wouldn't have an emotional melt down and become profoundly depressed to where she would die within two years of my father's death... that was the reported statistical survival rate of the elderly after the passing of their spouses. Each of us, his wife and children dealt with personal grief in different ways. My mother was initially very emotional and would cry often, sometimes remaining in her room all day long and not wanting to come out. I set her up with a small refrigerator and hot plate so she could snack when she didn't feel like coming out, but I would always knock on her door to see how she was doing. Initially, she slept a lot, but after about a month became more normalized and started to talk and come out for her regular routines. I thought how fortunate that we were able to celebrate her 81st birthday with my dad when he was still alive. It was a pity he couldn't have lived just two weeks more to have shared his 90th birthday with his family… that just wasn't meant to be. After 2 years being bedridden, he suffered from dementia and Parkinson's Disease, and died of respiratory arrest and a resultant heart attack from a morphine overdose administered by the hospice nurse. I suppose HMO administrators were happy my dad didn't incur costly ICU expenses that would be discounted by MediCare payments. This was probably a normal procedure for "compassionate dying" (killing) of elderly patients, all who would end up in prolonged and costly ICU care were they allowed to deteriorate to the state of impending death during the last days of their lives.

Perhaps if we had it all to do over again, he would have taken water with him on the day of his fateful walk. Perhaps he wouldn't have been such an old school stubborn man, and listened to my mother to seek help before he became dehydrated and likely suffered a mini-stroke. Perhaps had Kaiser staff treated him with due diligence instead of waiting 12 hours until my eldest sister intervened, his brain damage may have been reduced. Perhaps had the Hospice nurse not injected him with morphine the evening before his death, he might have lasted a bit longer. Perhaps. But he's been gone now for almost 5 years from October 23, 2008 and while we all miss him in our own personal ways, we think now of the positive contributions he made to our lives that instilled character and the will to live and achieve worthwhile goals. And above all, we know how his first priority was always to his wife, children and his dog Joy. I don't think we could have asked more of our father than what he was capable of giving, and what he in fact sacrificed and gave to each of us. Rest in peace Dad. God bless.

- Ingrid was an "au par" from Denmark who suffered silently with scoliosis.

She was the sweetest person anyone could ever be lucky enough to meet, yet get to know personally as a friend. She was absolutely great with children because anyone could tell she had a passion for loving them and caring for them was a well-honed skill she developed from taking care of younger siblings, as she was the eldest daughter in her family. I was occasionally substitute teaching Head Start nursery school kids for LACOE, and would call her for advice on how best to deal with some of the more difficult negative attention craving children from low income homes who tended to be somewhat boisterous, pushy, and inattentive to directions. She always had excellent examples of what best to do and what no to do, and her techniques were always effective, which certainly made my job a lot easier and more enjoyable when I could be more constructive and less frustrated with certain types of "ghetto" behaviors.

One day, I called her from work on my cell phone during my lunch break and another babysitter answered the phone, and told me Ingrid was not longer with them. I couldn't understand why she wouldn't be working there as she was happy, fulfilled and her employing family simply loved her to death. On further inquiry, the new sitter finally mentioned that the homeowner had mentioned that Ingrid had died from an undisclosed illness a week earlier and her remains were shipped back to her family in Denmark. I was shocked and literally dropped my phone, and as I picked it up to apologize, the new sitter had already hung up.

I felt guilty that I didn't know about her illness, that she never shared that with me. I had last visited her only a month earlier, and at that time, she had mentioned her back pain was getting somewhat unbearable due to her scoliosis and she was tired of taking Oxycontin for her pain. I suggested that she could ask her doctor for something else stronger, and she said there was nothing stronger that wouldn't be addicting, like

Heroin. I was bewildered. Did she try some bad street drugs and overdose? I didn't know her employer as they never knew we occasionally talked while she was babysitting, so I didn't feel they would even talk to me. It was rather inappropriate to ask personal questions that were on my mind about Ingrid, as that would never bring her back. I never had any contact with her family back in Denmark, so I was at a loss. I felt a hollow pit in my solar plexus... a yearning to hear her voice again... feeling incomplete from a sudden tragic loss. And there was nothing I could do about that to bring closure. I just knew in my heart, that if there is indeed a kind god (who allows wonderful loving people like Ingrid to suffer and die), then she must be in heaven for sure. But surmising that Ingrid was in a better place was unconvincing...

- Angel was a baby boy who was abandoned in trash bin by teen mother who I had met while teaching at a high school pregnant teen program.

The mom was an abused teen from a gang family. She had mentioned she was physically and sexually abused by certain unnamed family members and was eventually put into a foster care home where she was raped. She ended up hanging out with "hood rats" from her barrio and of course got knocked up by the time she was barely 14 by her gangster boyfriend. She came to school with a black eye once because her boyfriend claimed one of his "homies" saw her talking to another guy. Wow! She really deserved the beat down for that, right? And she being pregnant didn't seem to matter to her boyfriend, who after all was compassionate enough not to punch or kick her in her stomach, right?

She had mentioned to the class of eight pregnant teens that she would name her baby "Angel" because that's what she's always hope for in her life… to be saved by angels. I found out about baby Angel on television news when over the weekend, she was arrested for tossing her newborn into a trash dumpster. That Monday, when I reported to the classroom, I hoped and waited for her to show up, that the girl's whose photo I had seen on the nightly news was not Yvette. But her "home gurls" confirmed the bad news to me as several of them cried. One of the girls told me that she didn't want the child after her boyfriend beat her up and accused her of having the baby from another guy because the baby boy's skin tone was light and he had blue eyes. It's amazing how often ignorance can result in tragedy… most babies have lighter skin tone, hair and eye colors than when they mature. And in the case of Yvette, whose mother was a "Mulatta" or mixed with European ancestry, a random combination of genes could have resulted in a light skinned baby. Such a shame. I was really heart broken, as only a couple weeks earlier, we had a baby shower in the classroom for her as her "due date" drew near. She was so excited, though a bit apprehensive, and she looked forward to loving and caring for her boyfriend's baby. That all ended.

- Bernice was a very good mother by all accounts from people who knew her.

I met her when I was a manager trainee for a drug store chain and she was a check out clerk. At that time, she already had three young children who her mother babysat for her while she was at work, which explained the occasions that she reported late for work or had to leave early… which put her in bad light with the store manager. I usually covered for those times she couldn't be at work, so it really wasn't a big deal, but bosses tend to be rather rigid about schedules.

Bernice was feeling a lot of pressure from juggling work and her children. Her mother was also getting tired of caring for her kids, as her step-dad often complained that instead of taking care of "somebody else's kids" she should be working too. There was lots of family drama, and Bernice often seemed in a trance. One day she told me she was planning to quit work because after taxes, she was actually getting less pay than were she to go on welfare. She said once she had this baby, she would need to stay home for a while anyway, and welfare would pay her additional money. Once on welfare, she would receive free medical for herself and all her kids, instead of having to pay out of pocket since hourly employees didn't qualify for the company's medical plan at that time. In addition, she would qualify for subsidized housing, food stamps, school, and career training... and not have to deal with customers and an inflexible boss. I totally understood and sympathized with her position of being a working poor single mom. It's nothing I would wish on anyone.

I used to call her and her mom from time to time to ask why she wasn't at work, and the usual excuse was she was on her way. I chatted with her mom several times as she asked how Bernice was doing, especially when things started to get a bit dramatic in their family lives. She sounded like a patient, loving and caring parent, but I could sense a tone of frustration or desperation in her voice when we talked. A couple months after Bernice resigned from work, I called to find out how her new baby was doing, but she wasn't home. So I called her mother, who tearfully told me Bernice had lost her baby and she was in jail. That didn't make one bit of sense, so I asked, "What?" Her mom explained that Bernice had postpartum depression, and one day while shopping on a very hot summer day, forgot her new born was strapped to a car seat on the passenger side of the car, and didn't notice her baby while getting out of the driver's seat. She was only running inside a drug store (ironically the same drug store chain) to pick up her prescription for depression and wasn't gone but maybe 15 to 20 minutes... but by the time she got back to her car, her baby was dead. She called 911 for help, but afterwards the police arrested her. That story was very disheartening, and hearing her mother sob and knowing what a good mother Bernice was, as a patient and pleasant person who tried to please people, it was just a bit too much. Life just wasn't fair. Where was god when she needed him?

- Kenny was a good drinking buddy of mine who I had known since college dormitory days as my roomie.

In fact, it was he who introduced me to beer, Red Mountain wine, and marijuana. He was a good kid and loyal friend who grew up in a solid upper middle-class family who lived in Malibu's idyllic Broad Beach neighborhood. I once dated his sister a couple of times and took her to her Disneyland Grad Night when she was a senior at Santa Monica High and I a freshman at UCSB. Those were the good ol' days for sure... just good times and no responsibilities.

Kenny and I kept in touch off and on through out our adult years, and I'd occasionally check in with his sister Maggie, who was married and had two kids. Kenny never got married, but bounced from gal to gal... as long as the good times were there, he'd stay. But when the drama started up about getting married, he bailed. He never had any kids because he was a grown-up kid who still saw the world as a place to have fun, party, surf, camp, and hang out. I think maybe it was because his dad died when he was in college, he decided to drown his sorry with good times instead.

32

We lost touch for about a year as Kenny was an adventurer and the last I had heard, he was in Australia, Catching some waves and hanging out in the Outback. One day, Maggie emailed me to let me know Kenny had died from

liver failure, probably due to excessive alcohol consumption. He was back in Malibu because he was feeling ill while in Australia. She stated that it wasn't more than a month when he returned looking weak and jaundiced that he died while in the hospital. Maybe he knew he was seriously sick... it's likely his liver pain was excruciating toward the end. But Kenny would be the first to deny it... he was an outdoor type who had many bumps, bruises and several broken bones in his life, and he never let any pain stop him from pursuing the good times, mostly drinking and partying with his surfer chums.

I felt badly that I didn't attend his funeral. I felt really badly for Maggie, as within the past decade, she had lost her sister Cathy to suicide, her mom to breast cancer, and now her oldest brother. Her dad had passed away when she started college at Santa Monica College, but now she only had one sibling left, David, who was a cop in Riverside. I don't know why I didn't muster up the stuff I needed to attend Kenny's funeral... I called Maggie a week later to apologize. She said she was a bit disappointed that I didn't show up since she knew what good friends her brother and I were at one time. I explained that I was still in disbelief, and were I to attend Kenny's funeral, I was afraid I might have had an emotional meltdown in front of his surfing buddies. I suppose I still wanted to hold on to my fond memories, and not face the truth that I would never see him again. Since then, Maggie and I got together briefly on the first anniversary of his death at his gravesite. It was a very touching moment, as we hugged and cried.

- Casey and Charleen were a perfect couple who were made for each other.

They were always together like the "Bopsy twins" and were always happy, smiling, laughing and doing everything together. They even wore "his and hers" fashions, that I thought was so funny at times. Well, at the least, they were always color coordinated to match, haha. I met them by fluke of luck when I moved next door to them. I was married at that time, and he had a large back yard garden that I could see over the block wall. They were always very neighborly and Casey often offered to help me with my yard or house repairs, while Charleen was a great hostess and cook, and they would invite us over to their house on a monthly basis for dinner.

They were both getting along in age, being in their 70's when I first met them. But Charleen was always out there watering her rose bushes and flowers that surrounded her house front and back. Casey loved to garden and taught me how to take care of plants. He always said, "Treat 'em like they're your kids, and they'll be healthy and give you back ten folds what you put into them." I found that to be good advice.

He let me plant vegetables in his garden that we shared. The first time I bit into a fresh tomato off the tree, my taste buds just lit up as never before! Eventually, we ate fresh veggies like several types of squash, string beans, and even watermelon and cantaloupe! The difference between tasting and eating fresh veggies filled with the juices of life, versus the pesticide laden dead month old vegetables from the supermarket was like night and day.

I would have to say, they were the happiest couple I'd ever met in my life! Unfortunately, the cruelty of life comes along with the wonderful moments... and one day the paramedics came for them – both of them! I talked to their eldest son who visited them weekly, and I had mentioned I didn't see them out an about for about a week, even knocking on their door a couple of times. I figured they had gone to visit one of their kids, which they did from time to time, as Casey could still drive. His son Aaron told me that when he came by for his weekly visit, no one answered the door, so he let himself in with his entry key. He was shocked to find them both in bed, peacefully hugging each other to the end. Aaron said they had come down with the H1N1 flu together, and both died in their sleep from pneumonia. As an autopsy wasn't done due to the apparent natural death, we will never know if they both died at the same very instance, or if one died first, and the other soon followed. They were ol' school and didn't like going to doctors for what they likely figured was just another bad cold, so I doubt if they received any medications or antiviral drugs like Tamiflu.

I attended their funeral in Rose Hill Memorial Park. It was a very somber and reflective memorial for two of the best people I've ever met in my life. They were simple, up front, honest, kind, caring, and good-natured. Maybe god wanted them in heaven to give them their just rewards. That's what I wanted to believe. Their house was put up for sale and sold within a month during a hot real estate market period. The new neighbors where "Yuppies" who ripped out all the flowers and garden, and I overheard them stating that "hicks" must have lived in this house before they bought it. I felt like yelling at them over the back yard wall to correct their offensive stereotyping statements. I wanted to tell them that Casey and Charleen were ten times the people these new neighbors could ever hope to be... but then realizing my new show off materialistic neighbors wouldn't care to hear that, so I kept it inside and decided never to introduce myself to them because these new neighbors would be so pale in comparison to the humanity that was always shown by Casey and Charleen. I really miss them.

- Claus was a middle-aged neighbor from Germany who choked on Bratwurst at restaurant.

Being a rather large guy, no one intervened to help him when he started grabbing his throat, then got up and staggered around before turning pale, then falling across a table of food and knocking everything over on to other guests. It was a real

mess. But the sad thing was all he really needed was some one to give him the Heimlich Maneuver, but unfortunately, his wife and teen kids who were eating dinner with him didn't know anything about First Aid methods. He died horribly and needlessly in front of his entire family. There was lots of screaming, crying, and drama with everyone standing around helplessly, even with his son slapping him on the back of his shoulder, the meat was not dislodged. While I wasn't present, this is the story that his son told me a month after I attended Claus' funeral at the Forest Lawn in West Covina. He was a well-respected and loved husband and father, and a good neighbor who would give his shirt off his back to help out, loan tools and equipment, and even knock on my door to warn me to move it off the street to avoid street sweeping tickets.
The real odd sight many customers saw was Claus trying to down a large stein of beer to wash down the stuck sausage, but other people just thought he was guzzling too much beer and becoming falling down drunk. Very sad indeed.

- Paul was a college classmate who was working on his AA degree in Corrections, with a concentration on juvenile justice.

He had a passion for this field because he had been incarcerated for a couple of months as a teen at a boot camp in Lancaster for stealing a car for a joyride. During the flu season of his sophomore year, he came down with a nasal infection after a brief rain that brought down all the allergens. He sounded all plugged up and had difficulty breathing through his nose, but he said he didn't have flu symptoms. He just complained about having headaches and a stiff neck. Paul didn't have a medical plan, as he worked part-time at a local Carl's flipping burgers next to campus to earn money for his rent and books. He thought his illness was just another occasional cold, and since he couldn't afford to visit the doctor and medication, he just figured he'd get over it. But the cruel and unexpected act of fate spread his nasal infection to his brain, and his roommate had to call 911 when he found Paul collapsed in the bathroom. I heard that he died from complications due to bacterial meningitis, at the age of 19. What a waste of a good guy.

- Bryan aka Caspar was of 4th generation German heritage, and an accomplished surfer who had surfed since he was five years old.

He was fearless and would go out on days even seasoned surfers would otherwise watch the water. He loved to go up and down the coast of California whenever a storm promised big waves. He was born in Huntington Beach – the official Surf City, and watched all the best of his time in competition. While he never reached the top competitive level, he was well respected by other surfers and rarely had to fight over turf as his reputation for good rides and being a nice guy who could hold his own had eventually preceded him. He was a local legend of sorts, and was also known as a good grappler, so most guys didn't bother to test him and his crowd. During a huge storm that pounded the coast, he decided to surf Mavericks at the break of dawn, alone because his buddies told him he was crazy and it was too dangerous. Later that morning, his buddies decided to go down to see if he indeed was out in the waves, but after seeing his parked truck, they didn't see a sign of him. They reported this to the Life Guard station, and a search was started. Unfortunately, his body was found a mile up the coast, and apparently he had drowned after being smashed by a big wave and kept submerged in the under toe. I knew his girlfriend, Minmay (she had big eyes like the cartoon), who was torn apart by his sudden and unexpected death. She blamed herself for not trying to stop him from leaving that morning, but she was a bit hung over from the previous night's bash. I told her it wasn't her fault, and at least, Caspar died doing what he most loved. Little consolation, I know.

- Katie was a middle-aged wannabe mom who couldn't conceive.

After a decade of infertility and approaching 35, she and her husband decided she should try fertility treatment because her husband's sperm was still fertile. After a couple of months, she conceived and they were undoubtedly at the moment receiving confirmation of her pregnancy, she was the happiest person on Earth.

She felt quite ill the first couple of months of her pregnancy and spent most of her time in bed, getting up to use toilet often for nausea. But after a while, she adjusted to the growing babies inside her body and would have to pinch herself to make sure she wasn't just having vivid dreams about it as before. Her husband really babied her, and served her hand and feet. She felt like a queen, but more importantly, she felt "alive" for the first time in her life! Around five months, she began to feel lots of activity in her womb... much movement. But the doctor did an ultrasound and said everything looked okay, and they were just probably moving around. She stated sometimes in certain positions or when "kicked" in a certain area, she would feel a dull pain, but it was really noticeable a few times. She was having some severe pain one evening, and her husband called 911... she felt like the babies wanted to come out already, four months ahead of the due date! The EMS got to her within minutes and checked her vitals as she complained of a severe pain in her stomach. She began to get a bit hysterical, but the paramedics allowed her husband to be in the vehicle for the ride to the hospital, so he comforted her somewhat as she repeated stated her worries about her babies dying... that she had a dream something was wrong and so on. The EMS admitted her to the Emergency Room, and the doctors knew right away something was wrong as she was hemorrhaging through her birth canal. They rushed her to surgery, but several hours later, she died in premature childbirth due to a uterine rupture during. The doctors were not able to save her 6 fetuses, who died with her. Her husband was so distraught that he had to be sedated and admitted. My doctor nephew hear this story from one of his colleagues who shared

practices in a fertility treatment clinic, and mentioned that while this was the worse case scenario, in over 90 percent of the cases, everything turns out fine and without any complications. Some consolation.

- Let's call her Jane Doe... a newborn infant without a name who died from asphyxiation with a plastic bag. The mother was a college student who got pregnant at a Frat party and was trying to hide it from her parents. She obviously was with baby, but her roommate girlfriends were excited about that a highly emotionally supportive. They also felt a little guilty that it was they who convinced her to attend the Toga party at the Frat house, fully knowing the boys would "spike" the punch. Her girlfriends didn't know she was a "lightweight" when it came to drinking booze. Of course, the fruit punch had been mixed with several bottles of vodka to help move the party along, and action into the bedrooms. And it wasn't long before Stephanie was butt naked under an athletic jock frat member. She later testified that she didn't remember who she had sex with because she became unconscious from the punch. When asked why she wrapped her newborn in a trash bag and tossed it into a trash dumpster in her apartment complex, she said she felt confused and didn't want the infant to grow up without a father, and she couldn't take care of it and still complete school. But most of all, she would have to return to her parents home for summer vacation, and she didn't feel she could endure the moral scolding she would likely receive from her parents, particularly her Mormon father who was well respected in his church. I read this as a news story, and it was shocking that a middle-class college coed could be so stupid and heartless. But after discussing this story with several friends over the following week, we mostly agreed that she killed her baby because she feared her father's wrath more, and she was still somewhat innocent, immature and obviously confused by some of her Bible readings. After she became pregnant, she was known to quote verse to her galpals, such as "*I will ask for wombs that don't give birth and breasts that give no milk*" (Hosea 9:11-16 NLT), but her roomies thought that was just self-talk to calm herself.

- Jenny was a 12 yr. old girl who was raped and killed while home alone during a home invasion robbery. Jenny's single mom worked after dropping her off at school early in the morning several hours before school started. Jenny would sit at the lunch benches waiting for the bell everyday for classes to start, then to get home at 4 pm, she would walk a mile along a major street that led to one bed room apartment that her mom rented in a lower-middle class neighborhood. It appeared that on her last day walking home, a couple of guys followed her home and when she opened the door, they forced her inside. It was reported by neighbors that a couple of teenaged boys around 19 years old had been seen riding their bikes away from the apartment complex that afternoon, but there was no security footage since this low income apartment community didn't have security cameras.

Forensic evidence showed that Jenny struggled for her life as she was violently raped, struck repeatedly, kicked, and apparently held down by one teen while the other raped her, possibly taking turns. She had lost an eye in the beatings, had concussion injuries, and vagina hemorrhage and a broken arm. She was finally stabbed more than a dozen times with a large kitchen knife typically found in most homes that was apparently taken from the kitchen. Her puncture wounds included a collapsed lung, punctured kidney, lacerated stomach, large and small intestines, and a punctured heart. Her vagina was also split open several times, but it wasn't clear if those injuries were inflicted before or after she died from any of several wounds sustained. Years later, this is still a cold case that may never be solved. It was so shocking and disgusting that the Chief of Police broke down and cried during a news briefing, and he promised never to give up looking for the murderers, but still no progress. The crime scene was exceptionally gruesome, and it's probably likely the boys were high on meth, as the level of violence would suggest that. Jenny's neighborhood was infested with meth addicts and sexual predators, with more than a dozen sex offenders living within a 5-block radius of her apartment.

- Dixey was an outdoor hiking and camping fanatic. He was raised in the Appalachian mountains among "hill people" and was one of very few who left their familiar clan environments to venture outside to the chaos of the modern world, but his departure wasn't of his choosing. His dad was a traditional no nonsense drunk and abusive man. He was portly and as the head of his clan, he was both feared and respected. Dixey's trouble with his dad started when he turned 16 and his drunken dad was throwing his mom a very bad beat down, worse than normal. His mom screamed for help, and Dixey mustered up all the courage he had to jump on his dad in an effort to pull him off his mom. But his dad was too strong and wide to take down, and what resulted was a beating that left Dixey with several cracked ribs, a dislocated shoulder, and a fractured jaw. Dixey wasn't allowed to get medical attention, so his mother did her best to bandage him up. While Dixey's dad felt kinda sorry he had hurt his oldest son so badly, he had to remind Dixey who the boss was in their house.

From that point on, Dixey thought to escape his miserable life. A few years later on his 18th birthday, he hiked out of the hill country and caught a few rides by hitchhiking to the hills of western North Carolina, where he managed to live off the land and small animals for several years. Dixey was quite resourceful as he hunted and foraged for his subsistence lifestyle with his large Jim Bowie knife that almost all Appalachian boys were proud to possess as indication of their manhood. He had built a shelter from small trees and branches, and used leaves to provide cover and shade. His shelter was well camouflaged as a dugout against a hill, next to a small trickling stream from higher elevations. He made a fire pit with large   stones just outside his shelter, and made an elevated roof over his fire pit to keep the rain and snow from knocking out his fires, and that helped to keep him warm through the winters. Unfortunately, during an especially cold but clear winter night, his fire got out of control as he slept and hot embers lit his shelter on fire. He apparently woke up at some point, but his burning shelter collapsed on him and he became tangled up in the burning branches and got 3rd degree burns over half of his body. The fire eventually spread up the hill and was noticed by the fire service lookout tower ten miles away. When the fire fighters got to the scene, Dixey was already unconscious and still smoking, but barely alive. He was air lifted to a burn center in Charlotte, where he succumbed to his injuries a week later. No one claimed his body, and it was cremated. It was a real shame that this boy lived a highly abused life, and when he sought freedom and tried to make the best of his life that an illiterate person can do in our modern society, he was dealt yet another card of fate… the Ace of Spade…DEATH.

- Kimmy was a wonderful wife and mother who died of cervical cancer at the age of 45.

She got married when she was 15 because her family was very poor, and that was a way for her to get out of poverty. Her husband was kind and hard working, and together they had 3 kids, a boy and two girls. They were both very happy that all of their children ended up with college degrees and became successful in different careers of their choice. Their fortunes had been blessed by a booming real estate market, and a house they had bought for only $35,000 two decades later increased its value ten folds. Kimmy and her husband sold their house and bought a used deluxe motor home for $60,000 so they could travel the country. They had enough cash left to retire from their jobs. Everything was rosy, and Kimmy often looked back on her impoverished childhood and thanked God for sending her a good man who loved her to death. Kimmy noticed her menstrual period was becoming irregular and there was occasional bloody discharge between menstruation, but she thought it to be part of menopause due to her age, so she never mentioned it to her husband or children. She thought se would get over it in time when her hormones leveled off as she got over menopause. It was on one especially long cross country trip from the East Coast to the West Coast during winter that she felt odd and noticed an especially large amount of vaginal discharge. They checked her in at an emergency room on route, and she was given a blood test and vaginal swab. The lab results came back with horrible news, that she had HPV, one virus thought to cause cervical cancer. As she and her husband were still relatively young, they didn't bother to purchase a medical plan, and only had catastrophic coverage insurance. They returned home and she underwent treatment, however, with the high co-pays and the expensive chemotherapy, they were rapidly becoming broke. She opted to continue traveling with her husband and discontinued chemo because she wanted to die doing what she enjoyed the most, and being in the arms of who she loved most of her life. One evening while they were parked at an RV resort near Laughlin, after a wonderful day on the river and in the casinos, she laid down next to her husband that night, kissed him and told him she really loved him and could never love another man as she had loved him. She said she was blessed to have him in her life. She told him she looked forward to making him his favorite breakfast the next day, Valentines Day. She wanted to try a new recipe for a special Valentine's chocolate cake she found in a Paula Dean cookbook. He told her he couldn't wait. After she fell asleep, her husband went to their car and brought in 3 dozen large fresh roses and a heart shaped box of Sees Chocolate and placed it in the in front of the mirror in their bedroom so that would be the first thing Kimmy would see when she woke the next day. But as fate would have it, she died peacefully in her sleep.

Chapter 6 –My sadness, sorrow, despair and hopelessness

How Badly and Sad I Felt About Deaths in my Rabbit Family

My personal experience with profound depression began gradually, and I didn't recognize the symptoms of the transformation of "normal" occasional sadness into deep-rooted depression. I had been a fairly content and happy child, who dealt with occasional violence from bullies, but did well in school to validate my self-worth. I had been more of a loner than sociable because my younger brother ""stole" my best friend when I was 12, and my neighbors were horrible kids who were violent and I had to regularly fight them off.

It wasn't until I unexpectedly raised bunnies left to my care by my irresponsible live-in gambling addicted girlfriend that I found myself absorbed into the daily lives of other sentient living beings. Over time, I became a dedicated parent to an ever-growing tribe of rabbits and raised babies until they were 2 months old before I gave them up for adoption. I kept the adults, and their ranks began to increase as I became more attached to more and more rabbits due to my daily care.

I observed them daily, interacted with them beyond just feeding them, and became concerned for their illnesses and saddened by their deaths, even after lengthy medical treatments that couldn't spare their lives. Over the six years that I cared for my rabbit tribe, I cradled at least a dozen bunnies in my arms as they took their last breaths from irrecoverable illnesses. I witnessed some from my dear family of bunnies suffer various illnesses, struggle to survive, and after much expense and dedicated medical care that I gave to them at the direction of veterinarians, they still died. It was horrible, and with each death, I felt something die inside me. I cried for each rabbit that died, including those few who died from various accidents, such as getting cut by a hidden fence shard while attempting to escape their pens. I wanted death to stop taking my dearest, but it would regularly revisit me.

- Lovely Igor – wryneck – ear infection. I felt guilty that I should have taken her to the Vet at the beginning instead of assuming she has scoliosis. After reading on the Internet that she may have had an ear infection, I waiting another month before doing anything – and only after she seemed to be doing poorly, near death. Had I intervened much earlier, she may have gotten well and survived. I always felt badly that she may have been in pain and suffering while displaying such gentleness and affection toward me and the little ones that she babysat. I will never forget her tenderness. I felt very badly that she used to look at me when I gave her the nasty tasting antibiotics and seemed to be asking me, "Why are you killing me daddy? I love you!" I miss her dearly as I had nursed her back from death twice, just to lose her at the end. She was barely alive and I had to bag her and holding her, watched her take her last breath. It was very sad and before she died, I showed her to her parents and brothers… then I buried her along side Angel Baby who she may have accidentally killed when having a convulsion and fell on him (or maybe he died due to malnutrition, lack of Brownie's milk and didn't eat pellets). Anyway, I felt deeply sad to my soul that I did not do the right things that would have saved her earlier on.

- Pollie – Pasteurella. I was not particularly close to Pollie, but I saw him grow up as part of the twins (Rollie and Pollie). I felt very badly that he also looked at me and tried to get away from being forced to drink antibiotic and having nasal spray up his nose. One day I came home as he didn't seem to be getting better – very difficult breathing – and he was hard, on his side and with ants all over him in the garage. I cleaned him up, triple bagged him and put him in the trash bin. I felt very sad, as he was a good rabbit and never fought or made trouble with other rabbits.

- Kenny – alcohol diarrhea – I was high on booze and thought it would be cute to chew up some carrots with beer and feed it to him via my mouth... he loved it and sucked it up. But 3 days later, he had diarrhea... and I was playing with him by stuffing him and Kimberly down my shirt... Kimberly came up for air, but Kenny stopped moving. I gave him mouth to mouth several times, and he almost took a breath... but then died. I felt very guilty and like a stupid fool for doing these irresponsible acts that killed him. He was so frisky and sweet. I missed him for an entire week, lamenting on my stupid alcohol driven actions.

- Baby Amberly – dropped – diarrhea – I picked her up to pet her as I was sitting on a stool, but she was so scared and frisky that she scratched and leaped out from my hands and fell on the kitchen floor on her stomach making a loud flop sound. 3 days later she had very bad diarrhea and when I came back from work, I found her rigor mortis body lying on its side in the kitchen as other rabbits avoid her.

- 9 babies due to heat wave – Brownie's first born... this was both a freak of nature and stupidity. Brownie had decided on the space under the stove to have her babies – and I wanted to make it comfy for her and the babies, so I ripped up a polyester pillow and put pieces under the stove for their nest. They survived the first day of the 105 heat wave as we had the AC on, but the next day Suzy left for school without turning on the AC and when I got home from work, I noticed Brownie was in the kitchen with her ears shaking and wiping her face over and over. I used a mirror to look under the stove and all of her 9 babies were dead – hardened and tangled up in the polyester fibers. I removed all the dead babies, cleaned out the polyester and Brownie's fur, and vacuumed. Brownie revisited her den many times over the next 3 days and cried over and over. It was very dramatic – but Suzy laughed and said she acted like the 3 stooges when constantly wiping her face with her paws. I felt very badly for Brownie that her babies would otherwise had survived if the AC was turned on, and instead of hot and tangling polyester fibers, we had put in pieces of cotton towels. Big mistakes.

- 5 babies Brownie decided not to feed due to ants – She had the babies under the desk in the living room and 4 were still together in a group, so I gathered them and placed them in a flat box cut out with timothy hay and put them and Brownie in the bathroom and she seemed to adjust and was nursing them. The next day, I found a 5th baby that wandered from under the desk and was in the middle of the living room with ants biting her all over her body. I washed her off and placed her with the other babies. I woke up in the morning to find that the ants were attracted to her and were chewing her up again, but also started to attack some of the other babies who grouped together away from the sickly one who wasn't being fed by Brownie. Once the ants started to attack the other babies, Brownie decided to reject all of them. I tried to get her to feed them, but she refused and they cried out for her, but eventually all died within the next two days, the last one gasping for breath and life in my hand. I scolded Brownie who hid her head under the sofa, and I bagged the babies and put them in the trash.

- 2 babies Brownie dumped on kitchen floor still in placenta because she didn't want to have any more babies feed on her. I was upset at Brownie that she could do that, but since the babies were dead already, I just bagged them and tossed them in the trash.

- 2 babies Brownie rejected once came out from kitchen cupboard den... Suzy grabbed one with her hand so Brownie refused to feed it.

- Angle Baby – flopped on by Igor convulsion – I had hoped it was going to survive and had an intuition I should separate him from Igor while she was having convulsions, but was rushing to work and found her dead in the cardboard living area when back home. I regretted once again not taking more proactive action based on my intuition.

- Killed by big black cat:
    1. Baby tan (Brownie) – I noticed it went missing but thought it was hiding in the den – I could find it for an entire week – and later concluded the cat ate it
    2. Baby gray (Brownie) – another mysterious disappearance overnight
    3. Baby Pixey (Pixey) – we release her back to Pixey's area after Catching her for sale, but she was cute so we decided to keep her – only to have Cat kill her later
    4. Baby Casper (Pixey) – Suzy's favorite perfect bunny was returned to Pixey and Casper but disappeared that very night and was found decapitated on neighbor's property.

5. Baby white (Pixey) – also disappeared

6. Baby Albino (Pixey) – found headless body trying to back into fenced area, but Cat had already ripped its head off…. It came back for it a couple of hours later (it ran off when we surprised it coming out in the morning at 6:30 am)

7. Baby light gray (Brownie) – one day it was there, and next day gone

8. Baby amber (Katie) – black cat ripped down unsecured plastic barrier, stuck paws in and ripped baby out through fence and chicken wire. I had planned to tie down the plastic barrier, but it got late and I got lazy, which cost a life.

- Wandered off or stolen - probably killed.

1. Little G – was born the evening my dad had died in the morning…. I thought maybe it was my dad's reincarnated soul. He was loyal to Whitie and I kept them together for the longest time. He was shy and mellow and didn't get into fights with other rabbits, but Whitie kept humping him and one day he beat up Whitie a little and I separated them. He was stolen from new

2. owner's front yard and I was sad to realize that he's probably dead. I later heard from Suzy that the woman's neighbor saw an old Chinaman put Little G in a bag and take him away – probably for dinner... Little G was probably happy thinking he recognized me and would get bananas, instead it was another Chinaman who probably treated on sweet banana-fed rabbit. I was both angry and sad... and if Little G was in deed my reincarnated dad, then I guess his soul will be reincarnated as someone else once released from G.

3. Baby Beige – was a bitch and terrorized Baby Whitie, which made him very fearful and paranoid. He also bit off half of Amberly's nose when I put him and Baby White with Amberly. I eventually put him by himself and he wanted to fight Ivory. He seemed to get along with Little G at Suzy's friends house, but it got away through the backdoor with Little G or was also stolen. After a week, he was returned or found his way home to new owner's front yard.

- Casper died of a heart attack while trying to escape from a large white container when I was moving him to the rest room for a bath. He had advanced Pasteurella and would probably have died within a few weeks if not sooner. When I gave him CPR, I could hear his lungs gurgling, and white discharge came out through his nose.

- Casper Jr. died of Pasteurella, chill and loneliness two weeks after Casper died. He was on his side having difficulty breathing and I put his food down for him then went to feed Dixie and minutes later turned around and Casper Jr. was dead, almost reaching the food.

- Katie almost died, but struggled to survive – aborted infected fetuses and lost weight. Still has problem with difficulty breathing and white puss came out of nose.

- Casey had 7 babies then Pasteurella difficulty breathing. I massaged her nasal passages to help her breath better. Not sure if she will survive to have second batch of babies and to nurse them like she is with her first litter.

In addition to the deaths of my dear rabbits, some of my close friends and relatives.

People I cared about who died
- Father – old age, morphine overdose
- George K – good kind friend, car accident
- Elaine Y – childhood classmate, lupus
- Uncle Tom – heart attack
- Aunt Georgina – lung cancer
- Grandmother Yin – cervical cancer
- Raquel B – drive by shooting
- Bruce P – heart attack
- Sandra M – galpal from suicide

While I was sad over the deaths of these close family members and friends, they were situations that happened when I was not present, and I learned about it after the fact. In some cases, their deaths were expected, but in others, death came as a complete surprise.

I mourned for each loss, but it hadn't impacted me as deeply as the deaths of my bunnies who I treated as my own children, all of whom I loved unconditionally as if they actually were my natural born children. Finally, I hadn't expected to have a near emotional breakdown after I gave away my last precious children to a rabbit rescue group to find them better homes, that due to financial reversals, I could no longer give.

My emotional journey with my rabbits, recorded by emails

Re: I miss my bunnies!

Blake Walker
Sep 15, 2013

To

heather@outlook.com

Thank you Heather for the pics and update. It was real hot yesterday, today and forecast for tomorrow so the RV is baking even with 2 window AC units running (the RV's are designed with a strong overhead AC for a reason, I've discovered, lol). I'm glad my bunnies were not here to suffer through it. I'm happy that they seem to have adjusted and are content and well cared for, with lots more room than they've had for the past 15 months since leaving my mom's house.

I was worried about Psycho falling down inside the pet carrier hard enough to crack the casing... I felt very stupid not to have taken down the carrier once I had put him inside and was trying to Catch Pink while getting the carrier for Amberly and Amber... it wasn't even a minute when I heard the crash. When I had kids, I dropped my son a couple of times, but caught him before he hit the floor, and my other son bounce off the bed when I jumped on it with him, but I grabbed his leg just in time before he hit the ground... several scares! Stupid dad, lol.

I've been feeling sort of empty with a pit in my solar plexus... feeling lonely like something is missing from my life. I know in time I'll get over this feeling, but it'll take time. I looked on the Internet to see if there are low maintenance pets that can stand the heat in my RV... only a land tortoise, but it turns out they shed salmonella bacteria, so if I don't wash my hands thoroughly, i can get food poisoning after preparing my meals. Since I've had the rabbits, i thought about getting a turtle, lol. I don't know what to do to find another pet that won't suffer in an RV, is sturdy against diseases, doesn't transfer disease to me, or require lots of time and attention once i go back to work full time. Do you have any suggestions? I think any animal, fish or bird would die in my RV heat in case of those unforeseen heat waves. So I don't know what to do... lizards aren't cuddly and snakes are a bit scary. I got so used to petting my bunnies and I miss that, and some of their antics.

Life is a trade off... I enjoyed watching my bunnies groom and love each other and I enjoyed feeding them because they were so eager to eat... especially when I had a few thin banana slices for them, they would stand up to beg for them, lol. But I'm not worrying about them anymore, or seeing them slowly deteriorate and get sick... everyone's poop except Psycho was getting smaller because they weren't getting enough exercise to move the food through their digestive tract... and I worried they would come down with stasis. So I'm relieved they are in much better environments so I won't have to worry about their health and possibly getting ill, suffering then dying like Dixey.

Well, I'm looking forward to doing lunch or dinner with you whenever you get a chance. I've started applying for full time work in my profession, but the economy hasn't recovered and jobs are still not abundant. Yesterday was a unique day for me, as I gave up my bunnies (children) to find better homes, and my daughter got married, but I wasn't there to give her away. I'm reminded how life never remains the same forever. Once I find a good paying full time job, I'll become a regular contributor to Humane. In the meanwhile, let me know if Cat thinks there's anything worthwhile in the proposal I had earlier sent you to raise spay and neuter funds for poor families. Or let me know if I can volunteer to help anyone with their bunnies.

I need to completely clean out my RV, take out the cages, spray everything down with anti-bacterial cleansers, vacuum everything (tons of dander everywhere, including the small particles and all lengths of fur... I can still see them floating around so I still wear my face mask for now). Once I get motivated to clean, I'll do it in stages because there's so much to do. One day I hope to meet some friends who love rabbits... not like my ex-gf who only liked to look at them if they're cute (her same standard for meeting guys, lol. she said old guys are ugly and she can get young men anytime she wants, lol). I have lots of pics, videos and some sound recordings of my bunnies, and one day I plan to make a DVD of their good times... and also a memorial to all those who died too young.

Well, I don't know how I can thank you for rescuing my bunnies from a certain ill fate if they stayed cooped up in my RV much longer. Once I become gainfully employed, I'd like to rent a room from a family with a house, yard and bunnies! And I will help them to take care of their rabbit family. Maybe if my situation improves before some of my bunnies get adopted, I can re-adopt them... but only if I live in a better environment with more clean air to breathe, have sufficient funds to pay for expeditious vet care, and have only spayed and neutered buns. I've learned my lesson the hard way, unfortunately my bunnies had to endure, suffer and even die needlessly because I wasn't smarter or had more money.

Thanks again for everything! Let me know if I can ever help you, Cat or Humane with anything within my capability and I'll try my best to do it. Hope to see you again soon.

Best wishes,

Blake

Sent: Sunday, September 15, 2013 4:45 PM

Hi Blake,

I hope you are relaxing a bit now that you don't have to worry about the bunnies! Attached are some photos - a few we took yesterday when we were letting the bunnies relax (after dropping BooBoo off to the other rescue), and a couple of Galbani and Miss Mustard that Cat had shown you on her phone, in their foster home. We gave everyone a nail trim, and will be getting everyone in for vet exams this week, likely, just to make sure all is well. We'll also schedule spays for the girls to help protect them from a reproductive cancer. I think they appreciated the opportunity to run around and stretch their legs - I know it was difficult for you to give them a lot of exercise time - we'll make sure they get daily run time so that they can build their muscles back up. They are all beautiful and good-natured rabbits. I seriously do not know how you managed all these months, keeping them and yourself alive. I find it challenging enough taking care of my bunnies in our house - it would be tough indeed to take care of them in a smaller space.

Thank you also for the cash donation and the extra supplies! We appreciate it!

Take care - I hope your health will improve now that you can have some extra space and less dust/dander to have to breathe in.

Heather

Hi Heather... Do you need the neutered certificates for Amberly and Psycho? Thanks again for all that you've done for my sweet bunnies. I will find a way to repay you for your compassion and kindness. Just let me know what you want that is within my capacity and I promise to do it for you. Please thank Cat for working with you to rescue my rabbits. I'm forever indebted. Best wishes, Blake

----

From: Heather

Sent: Saturday, September 14, 2013 8:09 AM
Subject: Re: drive into the driveway to the back

Thank you, Blake! We'll be there around 10, though we always tend to run late. :) I promise we'll take good care of the buns. We don't have space for any cages at this point, but I appreciate the carriers and other stuff. That would be great if you could go back to work now that the buns won't be weighing on your mind! Cat also has some photos of Galbani with his new girlfriend loaded on her phone, to show you. See you soon!

Hi Heather...

I'm ready for you. I washed the pet carriers and they're drying right now. I packed the hay into two large plastic bags. I have the 50 lbs of pellets in two bags. I also have a box of newspapers (mostly LA Weekly... free and perfect fit - but gotta remove the 2 staples first to prevent bunny injuries or ingestion).

I've given each of my bunnies extra petting this morning, but I don't
Know if they have a clue what's going on. I told them I'm going to miss
them, but they're headed for a better life. I'll try not to cry when I turn
their futures over to you this morning.

You can drive into the driveway... I'm in the far back with a red
blanket over my window. That way, I can load up your car with the other stuff
then get the bunnies so they won't get overheated waiting in the car.
While I'm loading your car, you can check out my rabbit set up with
cages and floor space, then let me know whether you think you can use me in an
emergency temp placement.

Thanks again for everything. I also want to make a donation to your rescue group,
though I know it's far from what expenses your organization will
incur for helping my bunnies find good homes. I'll try to make it up to
you someday, as I'd likely go back to work full time, now that I don't
have to fear my bunnies would suffer and die in the RV. Now we can do
lunch sometime and I don't have to worry about my bunnies roasting in a
hot RV. Just let me know when.

See ya,

Blake

From: Blake Walker
To: "heather@outlook.com"
Sent: Friday, September 13, 2013 8:09 PM
Subject: Re: We can take Booboo this Saturday

Sounds good Heather. If you don't care to see the cages, then I will get
the bunnies ready for transport and when you get here, you can drive
down the driveway so I can put all the bunnies in your vehicle, plus the
pellets, hay and newspaper . But if you want to see them inside my RV
in case you can use me as an emergency holding, I won't make any changes
for at least 3 months, I'll put them in the carriers at the last minute
after I load your car with the other stuff, okay? You can call me to let me
know which way you prefer. And if you leave your cell phone with me
again, then I can call you sometime to find out how I might be helpful
to you and/or Humane Pet Rescue. Thanks a million! Blake

From: Heather

Sent: Friday, September 13, 2013 7:58 PM
Subject: Re: We can take Booboo this Saturday

That would be helpful, Blake - thank you!

hi heather, i can put psycho and pink in one larger pet carrier and booboo in another. then all you need to bring is one carrier for amberly/amber, okay? Blake

---

From: Blake Walker
To: "heather@outlook.com"
Sent: Friday, September 13, 2013 3:38 PM
Subject: Re: We can take Booboo this Saturday

Hi Heather, Can you use a 3 ft. high stack of newspapers? How about 3 rabbit cages and 2 pet carriers? Thanks again... Blake

---

From: Heather

Sent: Friday, September 13, 2013 11:48 AM
Subject: Re: We can take Booboo this Saturday

Hi Blake, we will gladly take the pellets, and we will actually be able to take Psycho and Pink as well!! So, you should not have to stress about your bunnies anymore after tomorrow!! :)

Hi Heather... I would like to donate an unopened 25 pound bag of rabbit pellets (Furry Friends brand), and 25 pound bag of Purina Rabbit Chow (this is half bag remaining of a 50 pound bag) since I won't need it anymore. I'll keep just enough for Psycho and Pink. I have 1/4 bale of timothy hay left, but I'll keep it for Psycho and Pink and donate the rest when they are adopted out. Would you be able to use that for your rescued rabbits?

In the future, I'd like to periodically buy 50 lb. bag of rabbit pellets an a bale of hay for Humane and donate it for your use. I'm open to other ways I might be able to contribute to your bunny goals, only I don't know where I would best plug in. Here's my resume so you and Cat might see where I may have appropriate skills to contribute to your mission and vision. I remember my first contact with you was when I only had 6 rabbits (5 males and one female) and everything was in balance before all the uncontrolled births. At that time I had wanted to volunteer to help out at your Humane at the Pasadena Humane Society, but then they took away your space. It's ironic that my initial inquiry to become a Humane volunteer instead ended up with you rescuing my rabbits! It's strange how life works out sometimes. Had I not met you, and gotten some education through our emails and contact, I might have advertised my bunnies on Craigslist for uncertain and possibly negative outcomes.

Now, with you playing such an instrumental role in rescuing my bunnies and giving them a second chance at better lives, I can live with that and not feel guilty that I didn't do the right thing, and made yet more mistakes on their innocent lives.

Thanks for everything
and see you soon.

Best wishes,

Blake

From: Heather

Sent: Thursday, September 12, 2013 3:40 PM
Subject: Re: We can take Booboo this Saturday

Hi Blake, thank you! Is it okay if Cat from Humane comes with me?
And it looks like we'll be able to take Amber and Amberly this Saturday as well! I know it's supposed to heat up again so we are trying to get as many of your buns as possible so that you don't need to worry about keeping everyone cool. :)

Sure Heather. That would work out fine.

It's too bad Saturday's weather forecast is for 92 degrees, and not 82 degrees with earlier overcast like today, otherwise we could Catch breakfast before exchanging Booboo. Well, another time that is more convenient to you is fine. I'm willing to give you a tour of my RV (though it's somewhat shameful, I don't have much pride left so it will be okay), so you can see what limited conditions you're rescuing my bunnies from so they can enjoy a better life. You are doing them and me a big compassionate contribution to our lives.

That's why I want to help raise money to spay and neuter the rabbits that poor people have in their homes, and an education program to help them to be better and more aware parents to their pets (and kids, lol) that seems to be endemic to poverty and general ignorance of what is best practices in rabbit care.

Looking forward to seeing you again! Thanks again for everything.

Best to you,

Blake

From: Heather

Sent: Wednesday, September 11, 2013 11:35 AM
Subject: We can take Booboo this Saturday

Hi Blake, good news - one of our rescue partners can take Booboo -
Would I be able to pick him up from you this Saturday morning, maybe about 10 am?

Tx!
Heather

Blake Walker
Sep 16, 2013

To

heather@outlook.com

thanks heather! i'm still adjusting my emotions right now... i've cried everyday... can't get motivated to clean the RV yet... just been drinking, smoking, watching on-line movies, then sleeping, lol. i should be back to normal after about a week... that's my usual readjustment period to get over my "loss"... they were family to me, better than my real family, lol. but i know it's the best decision. once i get a few weeks down from where i'm at right now, things will become clearer on how i can contribute to saving bunnies through volunteer work...

From: Heather

Sent: Monday, September 16, 2013 8:14 PM

Hi Blake,

Thanks for the offer - there are a few pet-sitters locally who specialize in bunnies; I am not sure how high the demand is, vs. supply. I think most people have a normal number of rabbits (1 or 2) and just board them

---

with their vet or a rescue or a rabbit "b&b" since it's usually cheaper than having someone come out to their house. If people have a lot of bunnies, they are more apt to have someone come to their home, just for convenience sake and because it ends up being cheaper than boarding due to the volume.

I am really glad that you'll get to overhaul your place and that you'll hopefully be able to move around and breathe easier shortly! :)

Heather

Btw Heather, Do you think this bunny care and/or house sitting service for bunny lovers can be turned into a successful small business? Is there a need? I always felt when I had rabbits that I could never leave them alone because they needed to be fed fresh food at least twice a day, and temperature monitoring was always very important. I wonder how many rabbit lovers can actually get away for any period of time and not worry about their bunnies. Blake

---

From: Blake Walker
To: "heather@outlook.com"
Sent: Monday, September 16, 2013 8:40 AM

Btw Heather, I'm totally honest and won't go through people's homes, personal property, or invade their privacy in any way. I don't won't eat their food, drink their beer, tamper with their computers, go through their bedrooms or anything (except maybe use their toilet for an emergency). I can just go take care of their bunnies, then leave and lock up their houses. I was a Realtor for several decades, and I had many Open Houses... and NEVER one complaint or report of anything stolen by "Lookie Loos", so you, Cat and your volunteers can be assured that when they return home, everything will be exactly as it was when they left their house and bunnies in my trusted care. Let me know if I can ever provide this service. Blake

---

From: Blake Walker
To: "heather@outlook.com"
Sent: Sunday, September 15, 2013 9:56 PM

Hi Heather... I've got an idea how I can immediately help you, Cat and Humane. I can be a house sitter and bunny care provider for you, Cat and your volunteers in case they need to get away on the weekends... plus until i find a full time job, i can be available any day or several days in a row. I simply stay in their homes while they're away and take care of their bunnies the way they want. That also adds home security so it isn't empty for long periods. Well, let me know if anyone of your volunteers who house multiple rabbits needs this service... no charge to your volunteers. Thanks! Blake

---

Blake Walker
Sep 20, 2013

To

heather@outlook.com

Hi Heather,

Thanks again for the updated pics of Amberly/Amber and Psycho/Pink along. It looks like they're relaxed and have lots of room to exercise. I was just wondering how does the foster parents keep the Cats out? I had a big Cat problem when I had outside bunnies... it was daily vigilance and lots of high fencing.

Well, I'm feeling better now... I didn't cry yesterday and I'm down to drinking 4 beers instead of a 6 pack. I should be back to normal by Monday. Please let me know how you think I can help your rabbit rescue cause... I can help pick them up from distressed situations? Whatever is fine.

Let's do lunch sometime to discuss rabbit issues and how I can volunteer to help out in whatever way I am capable. I'm applying for work now, also looking out of state to lower unemployment areas like Washington, Texas, and Utah. Do you have any ideas of nice cities to live in, so I can look up the job situation there?

Thanks again for everything. You are a godsend. Let's keep in touch and not be strangers.

Best wishes,

Blake

Re: bunnies

Blake Walker
Sep 21, 2013

To   heather@outlook.com

Hi Heather,

I cried a lot today. i miss all of my bunnies and went down memory lane... too much needless suffering due to stupidity. i know i need to do right to bunnies. i want to help your cause. i promise to donate $50/month to Humane, and when I get a good job again, I will promise no less than $100/month. While on the individual level it's only a drop in the bucket... if we politicize a campaign to save our innocent rabbits from hunting, trapping, poisoning, beatings, research, breeding for food, abuse and needless slaughter, then I will do everything in my ability to help.

Thanks again for everything. Hope to see ya soon!

Re: bunnies

Blake Walker
Sep 21, 2013

To   heather@outlook.com

hi heather... i regret that dixey didn't survive long enough to find a good home. he was my only talking bunny... very sweet but very afraid...

From: Heather

Sent: Saturday, September 21, 2013 4:33 PM
Subject: Re: bunnies

Hi Blake,

I know you miss your bunnies - I'm so sorry this is difficult - any person with a heart would feel the same way, but I do hope you are comforted by the fact that the bunnies will be placed in great homes with families that will love them just as you do. Also, don't worry about bunnies being outside - the pics I sent were just of supervised exercise time, in a fenced-in area - the bunnies live indoors in an air-conditioned space, where no cats or other critters can get them! :)

Thank you for your generous donation offer; of course we can always use $ for vet bills and such, but please make sure to take care of yourself, first. As for livable cities - I've only lived up north in Berkeley, besides LA and Japan, so I don't have a great frame of reference. If I were to move, I would want to live somewhere fairly liberal and progressive as far as animal and human rights were concerned. I imagine I might like Portland, OR but don't know that I could tolerate the gloomy weather! I enjoy my blue skies.

We'll do lunch soon - in the meantime, take care of yourself!
Heather

P.S. I was just reading an article about all the merchants in West Hollywood upset over the ban on fur sales. I am floored that in this day and age, there is still such an appetite for fur coats and the like. Those animals - including rabbits - endure such horrific living and slaughtering conditions - all for an end product that is entirely just for vanity's sake. Ugh.

From: Blake Walker
To: "heather@outlook.com"
Sent: Friday, September 20, 2013 9:55 AM
Subject: bunnies

Blake Walker
Sep 22, 2013

To   heather@outlook.com

Hi Heather... Just for your records, Amberly, Ivory and Gorby are brothers, all born on July 8, 2008 to Whitie (who died on May 15, 2012, just before we moved to the RV). Whitie was born on January 2, 2008 and was brother to his wife, Brownie who was born on the same day. We had to give Brownie away around May 1, 2012 because I had to move out from my mom's house and give away all the rabbits that I couldn't take with me to my RV. He missed his wife too much and couldn't recover from his depression, thus refused to eat even though I fed him Oxbow emergency food. He was almost 5 and a half. Here's some pictures. My trip down memory lane was very painful... my bunnies and I have been through so much this past year... it was almost overwhelming. Thankfully, you and Humane rescued my dearest bunnies to give them better lives where they can be rabbits again. I'm forever grateful. Best wishes, and I'm looking forward to meeting you for lunch or dinner at a veggie place at your convenience. Blake

Blake Walker
Sep 23, 2013

To

heather@outlook.com

hi heather... i wanted to share some bunny pics of amberly, gorby and ivory when they were little bitty babies *:) happy they were so cute. also a few pics of them with their mom and dad. those were wonderful times just watching their closeness and antics. then they hit puberty and wanted to fight and rape. have you ever raised baby bunnies from birth? please feel free to email any pics to their new adopted parents so they will have some baby pics of their adopted bunnies. baby gorby was lighter when he was born... but he's the one with the white stripe on his forehead. thanks again for everything. Blake

Oct 2, 2013

To   heather@outlook.com

Hi Heather... hope all is well with you and your buns. It's taken me a bit more time to emotionally adjust to my bunnies being gone from my life, as I'm attempting to fill that void. But I'm feeling better now and trying to find my way to where I can be useful to the cause of rabbit rescue and eventual public policy changes to control rabbitries who raise bunnies for meat and fur, yuk!

Well, let me know if you might be available for lunch or dinner sometime after this weekend. I should be relatively back to normal by then and would like to give you a donation for Humane. Thanks again for everything.

Best wishes,

Blake

hi heather... hope all is well, but i surmise you're probably very busy with an overflowing plate. should you ever get a chance, could you let me know how the bunnies are doing? did any of them die? did ivory die when attempting to neuter? it would be nice if Humane could have an instagram with pics from adoptive parents to share how their rescued buns are doing. i would be able to see some of my babies in their new digs. i'm still looking for a volunteer opportunity, but don't know where to start. let me know if we can do lunch before thanksgiving when comet ison may crash into the sun and cause a power shut off emp from a super solar flare. thanks again for everything. Blake

On Thursday, October 3, 2013 8:21 PM, Blake Walker wrote:

Sound good Heather. Enjoy your trip. I'm very glad to hear my bunnies are still doing well. I hope their new fosters will email you pics someday that you could share with me. I'm looking forward to our get together. Thanks again! Blake
From: Heather
Sent: Thursday, October 3, 2013 8:12 PM
Subject: Re: future meeting

Hi Blake,

Sorry for not being more responsive - work has been crazy and I'm going out of town (for work, of course!) this weekend. So I'm pretty pooped!

Psycho and Pink, and Ivory and Pinky, made it safely to AZ. Amber and Amberly are still being fostered locally. I completely understand that it's been a difficult adjustment for you, but please know you did the right thing! :)

I'll email you next week when I'm back home and we'll figure out a date for a meal!

Take care,
Heather

Re: future meeting

> Blake Walker
> Oct 28, 2013

To

> heather@outlook.com

hi heather...

i'm sorry to hear of your losses and heart-wrenching work trying to save your pets... and all the work to take care of 20 rabbits. i wish you would allow me to help them when you feel overwhelmed or just need a break. i would enjoy that... i miss cutting food for them and sweeping up their poop, lol. it was a labor of love for almost 6 years and my greatest joy was giving them banana treats and watching them share food together... seeing them hug and groom each other and thinking how sweet it would be if i could ever have that from a human being, but it hasn't been in my destiny. of course petting them and cradling them in my arms was a treat (except when i cradled them while they were taking their last breaths was very sad and just tore up my heart).

i don't have any commitments so i'm totally open to your schedule for lunch. sure, cat is invited so i can again thank you both again for rescuing my dear bunnies, who i still miss so much... but i know it was the best for them, and also for my health too (though i still have lots of dander floating around from time to time in my rv, so i still wear a mask when sleeping and snoring).

72

i often think, had i not met you and got my perspectives straightened out rather than continuing to listen to my ex-galpal to please her, who started me on my $32,000 bunny journey filled with heartaches and heartbreaks, never once helping to care for them... i would still be breeding bunnies for sale. well that's in the past... i still feel very badly that i did a stupid and bad thing that was a great disservice to rabbits by not getting them all spaded and neutered from the beginning instead of listening to my unemployed and financially dependent galpal who wanted to sell bunnies for her income (which was not cost efficient as i spent ten times more on raising kits until they were 8 weeks old before i weaned them).

so now i want to do whatever i can to make up for my past mistakes and wrong attitude based mostly on ignorance but not evil intentions. i just don't know how and where to start. one day when i get back on my feet and have a yard for bunnies, i plan to adopt a bonded pair short hair bunnies, a siamese Cat, and a weiner dog from rescue groups and raise them all together. but that's going to be years off, cuz now i realize that i can't let them suffer for lack of proper vet care that cost money. my last experience was losing one of my fav bunnies after spending $700, but did not have the last $500 for the necessary operation to save him - dixey cuz my ex-galpal borrowed $400 after she had a break up with her latest guy pal who stopped supporting her, so she had no money to pay her bills. i'm such a dumb sucker for that selfish user. sometimes i just want to kick myself... hmmm, maybe i'll feel better if you kick me real hard, lol.

well, i've decided to apply for work. i stopped drinking beers and smoking medical cannabis, so my mind was clear enough to complete ghostwriting my fav uncle's memoirs. that made him happy. a month ago i almost got hired to work for the inner-city arts academy downtown, but when they called to schedule and interview and asked me a few pre-scheduling questions, i had been drinking beers and my slurred speech must have been obvious cuz they never called back, lol. oh well, i really didn't want to clear toilets and mop crap and pee off filthy disgusting student restroom floors anyway. so i just reorganized and shortened my resume and i'll be emailing it today to several positions looking for my type of skills and experiences. one pays $60K. hopefully i'll get hired. if so, i promise to be a monthly cash contributor to Humane. you will see i am a man of my word.

well, life is a journey, and i certainly must admit that even at my late age and after so much life experiences, my most important emotional awakening has been due to my love for my innocent babies who i will miss forever and ever. thanks again from the bottom of my heart for all you've done to help find my bunnies better homes. like i said before, just tell me what i can do for you, and i'll do my best to my abilities.

best wishes,

Blake

On Monday, October 28, 2013 10:36 AM, Heather wrote:
Hi Blake, sorry to be incommunicado - overwhelmed with work and sick critters - had to say goodbye to one of our elderly guinea pigs this weekend after several weeks of nursing care - in addition to nursing an

elderly bunny who is unable to walk and caring for rest of our 20+ animals. All your bunnies are fine - none have died! Sorry it's not always possible to provide updates. Galbani and Miss Mustard just got a new foster home that we hope might be a failure (as in, they decide to adopt them!) - I'll try to get updates on the AZ bunnies - stay tuned. Might have time for lunch this weekend or next - okay if Cat joins us? What day is good for you?

On Thursday, October 3, 2013 8:21 PM, Blake Walker wrote:

Sound good Heather. Enjoy your trip. I'm very glad to hear my bunnies are still doing well. I hope their new fosters will email you pics someday that you could share with me. I'm looking forward to our get together. Thanks again! Blake

---

Blake Walker
Oct 30, 2013

To heather@outlook.com

btw heather... just an idea. in addition to helping you or cat with your bunnies (if you want), i can volunteer to help dr. jones with custodial stuff like cleaning, office work, running errands like picking up supplies, and even helping with handling bunnies, starting once per week (of course i'm not qualified to be a vet assistant and that's not my intent to replace any of her help) even should i find a m-f f/t job in my career field of facilities management, i can still help on the weekends. i know she's been great in giving Humane discounts and donated services. and she was the one who saved brigit, my flem giant that you found a good forever home for. had i lived closer to her office, i would have taken dixey there and she could have saved him. the vets where i took him didn't even know his air passage was being choked off by the absess... and i had mentioned both the abcess and the gurgling sound that dixey was making. dixey saw 2 different vets there, and neither thought anything about those major observations... instead they said it was mites and fungus. what a pity. well, i guess we can talk about any potential role i could contribute when we meet. thanks. Blake

On Friday, November 15, 2013 1:08 PM, Heather wrote:
Hi Blake! Are you up for lunch tomorrow, Saturday 11/16 at 12:30? I think you had mentioned Happy Family on Atlantic (in that newish retail complex, right?) - that sounds good to us!

that's fine heather... let me know when ever is fine with me. sorry to hear about cat's bunny challenges. i wish there was a get rich scheme, but all the rich people run those scams... it's call ipo's with virtual firms that haven't turned any profits who suddenly become billionaires on wallstreet like facebook and twitter. i think maybe there's something that can be done to more aggressively seek donations to Humane... maybe write a grant and submit it everywhere? well, let me know if you need hand from time to time to care for the bunnies... goes for cat too. keep the faith. best wishes, Blake

Nov 16, 2013

To   heather@outlook.com

hi heather...

it was nice meeting you and cat over lunch... i forgot to give you your fortune cookies, lol. a strange thing happened when i got up to leave... the older woman who appeared to be the owner came and picked up my tab and tip, then went back to the kitchen. as i got up to leave, the two waitresses looked at me as if i was trying to skip out, and i had to tell them the owner took my payment. so i walked out as they stared at me, wondering if i was pulling a quick one on them. but i suppose the owner confirmed, because the cops didn't show up as i was walking to my car that i had parked on hellman, lol. i also forgot my take out food due to the almost drama. oh well.

i had the hay and newspapers in my car, so if you ever need it, i can drop it off to you. finally, if you or Cat need room for desperate bunnies, i can "foster" amberly and amber until someone wants to adopt them. i'm sure i can handle 2 bunnies with all my experience with them... and i can give them a lot more attention and do it right. let me know if either of you should get to that point that you need to make space. let's keep in touch. i plan to write a grant proposal for Humane before the end of the year. then we can identify potential grantors and start sending them proposals with the new year, if that's what you want to do.

if not, i will approach other rescue groups and try to form a consortium for political action and volunteer at other more traditional rescue groups who have facilities since i'm not needed under your local sanctuary model. btw, ever hear anything about ivory/pinky and psycho/pink? i read that booboo has a foster and nonose got adopted by his foster. who has amberly and amber? has anyone adopted that loving couple galbani and mustard? it would be great to hear about them and get some pics if anyone ever shares with you. thanks again for everything! *:) happy Blake

On Friday, November 15, 2013 8:10 PM, Heather wrote:
Hi Blake,

Thanks - maybe the hay and newspapers? Not too many, I think Cat and I are driving together and her car is small. :)

Yes, loss is unfortunately a major part of rescue - I have become much more philosophical about it than when I started - which is not to say that I am callous towards death, but rather that I know my focus needs to be on providing the best quality of life, for as long as possible, to any bunny I take in - and then facilitate a peaceful goodbye when the time comes. That can be as great a gift to the rabbit as providing a good life - allowing the rabbit to leave this world as quickly as possible once quality of life is no longer possible. And the passage of one, allows for the rescue of another in need.

To   Blake Walker

Hi Blake,

A belated thank you for treating us to lunch on Saturday, and also for the generous donation and gift card! I hadn't been to Happy Family since it relocated, and I have to say, everything we ordered was really good - some of the best Chinese vegetarian I've had in a while. :)

Thanks also for your willingness to help identify some grant opportunities for us. I hope you are not frustrated/upset by the fact that we are having difficulty pinpointing ways you can help us. Cat had mentioned that you posted on Facebook that we had not been responsive to your interest in volunteering, and to be honest, I was a little surprised and hurt that you would post that publicly. We are, it is true, selective about who volunteers for us and in what capacity - I cannot tell you how many times we have taken on new volunteers, only to have them flame out, or suddenly become disgruntled with us or another volunteer and then leave, or commit to more than they can reasonably take on, and then leave us holding the bag. Believe me, we appreciate that you want to help rabbits; however, at this time, given your living situation, it seems best to match you to volunteer tasks (such as grant research) that are realistic/manageable for you. I hope you can understand where we are coming from? You have talked openly about the impossibility of providing proper care for your rabbits, and it was a protracted situation that led to suffering for your bunnies and much heartbreak for you. So, I hope you'll agree that the best way for you to help rabbits now is to help us raise the funds needed for vet care for some of our high-need sanctuary rabbits, and for continuing to provide outreach and education to hopefully help people open their eyes regarding the need for spay/neuter, how to properly care for rabbits, how they are not good pets for children, etc.

Heather

Re: Thank you

Blake Walker
Nov 20, 2013

To

heather@outlook.com

76

Hi Heather,

I enjoyed our time together over veggie lunch... so you see, the 3rd time was a charm (the first two times we went to a non-veggie buffet), and I'm glad both you and Cat liked the food. I plan to go back today for their lunch special. Let me know if you ever want to Catch lunch again.

I'm sorry you felt surprised and hurt about my truthful comment on FB... I have a habit of not thinking "politically" and tend to just blurt out the truth, especially when I don't have the data to make informed decisions... kinda like what happened in my experience with my dear bunnies... learning by mistakes. While I plan to follow Humane and Cat on FB, I will refrain from making any future comments as there might be a chance my comments would not be appropriate for public consumption.

I totally understand your concern and perspective, "Cat had mentioned that you posted on FaceBook that we had not been responsive to your interest in volunteering, and to be honest, I was a little surprised and hurt that you would post that publicly. We are, it is true, selective about who volunteers for us and in what capacity - I cannot tell you how many times we have taken on new volunteers, only to have them flame out, or suddenly become disgruntled with us or another volunteer and then leave, or commit to more than they can reasonably take on, and then leave us holding the bag."

I am forever grateful to you and Cat for holding the bag on my bunnies. I will continue to help in what ways you feel are appropriate, and even though I don't cut sufficient mustard according to your organizational plans, I hope someone will adopt Mustard and Galbani, lol. This is not the first or last time that I have been an unchosen suitor, as I've become accustomed to rejection since I resigned from my job in 2009 to devote all of my time to raising my bunnies, and then could not get hired back into the job market after so much time off and getting older. It is what it is.

I would like a clarification of the type of grant proposal you are looking for, that you feel would stand a greater chance of funding. Following is my unconfirmed suppositions:
- you need funds for veterinary care for illnesses, spay/neuter for bunnies that are/will be domiciled in your sanctuary network model.
- extra money for bunny care... food/pellets/hay.

After I had presented my unpersuasive pitch on my rabbit activism ideas to ban almost anything bunny except for rabbit rescue, I will not include any political statements or positions in regards to the Executive Summary in the grant proposal for Humane. But thank you and Cat for listening to such extreme ideas. I will also scale down the funding proposal by a factor of ten, to request modest funds in the range of $10,000 for which I am not requesting any fundraising fees. This will be my temporary and voluntary role with Humane, as I plan to write broader and larger grants in the future that I will pitch to other organizations whose passion is to promote an animal rights political agenda, or who desire to build rabbit sanctuary facilities. I hope at least some of my future work will be successful, but like everything else in life, the odds of success are not promising in a recessionary environment teetering on the collapse of the dollar.

If you feel we have a mutual perception on my role, please let me know if you and Cat agree and I will proceed. If not, please clarify your position so I can try to maximize any potential benefit I might bring to Humane. I will try my best according to the need(s) that you delineate. Well, with Thanksgiving just around the corner, and Comet Ison reaching perihelion on Thanksgiving Day, we may indeed have some awesome sights to view during this holiday season. I hope you will all enjoy your festive times with family and friends, as I'm sure you have at least 20 rabbit reasons to be thankful.

Grant Proposal

Blake Walker
Nov 21, 2013

To

heather@outlook.com

Hi Heather,

Attached is the preliminary grant proposal to address your organization needs as explained to me during lunch with Cat. Please review it at your convenience and make any corrections you deem necessary. I created the proposal using PowerPoint to give you the additional flexibility of giving this proposal as a slide presentation to potential grantors or other audiences.

This proposal is missing a cover letter and signature page, but I can provide that should you decide to proceed with this effort. If you give me the green light, I will identify likely donors from grantor databases and forward that information to you. Subsequently, you could print the final hard copies and submit them to appropriate donors.

Good luck and Happy Thanksgiving!

Blake

Heather
Nov 23, 2013

To

Blake Walker

Hi Blake,

Sorry for not responding yet - my big work event was this Thursday night, so it's been a crazy week and now I'm in recovery. :) I'll review everything you sent - thank you!

Heather

Blake Walker
Nov 23, 2013

To

heather@outlook.com

Hi Heather...
I hope you received the draft of the grant proposal and will have time to review it and make changes as needed. I don't really know much about Humane besides what I found on the FB pages and HUMANE webpage, so you may want to add organizational background stuff. A cover letter, grant cover page listing the donor information, and an organizational submission page with Cat's signature will be needed before the grant proposal can be submitted.

I also wrote to PETA and ASPCA for referral information and they both have many political activism projects in play all the time. I'll see how I might fit into their various outreach programs, though I would have liked to do more on a local level, but that doesn't seem practical or available at this time.

I also want to clarify my short inquiry on Cat's FB page... I was responding for her call for volunteers when I stated that I had previously inquired on FB but didn't get a response. In reply, Cat suggested that I would send her a message and she would let me know who to contact, which I did. So just for your information, she did not respond to my message either, and instead I received an email from you the very next day stating you felt surprised and hurt. I had also emailed Dene at Humanevolunteers@gmail.com twice in addition to my FB inquiry, and no response. But in order to avoid possible controversial statements, I'm no longer following Cat's page, so no need to worry about public statements. And I will no longer inquire about volunteering for Humane. Of course my invitation to help you stands, though I doubt you will take me up on it.

When I don't get any response, I eventually conclude there's no interest. That's okay... I accept it. I don't want to persist and be seen as a stalker. I must recognize that I'm probably viewed negatively due to mistakes I've made in raising rabbits, primarily due to my lack of rabbit care knowledge. But in all fairness, had I received a more timely education on rabbit care, I supposed I could have prevented my male bunnies from digging under the fences into the female bunnies' segregated areas (never thought they would or could do that). Had I more money for vet care, I would have spayed and neutered all my dozen rabbits before they ended up reproducing. Had I received tips on proper feeding and sheltering strategies, I could have avoided excess expenses for veggies along with preventing Cat predatory kills. Mistakes are the dear cost of ignorance and stupidity, and hopelessness the consequence of poverty.

While I viewed Internet articles, no site presented an "ideal pro-active" strategy for rabbit care and prevention of negative outcomes. They had plenty of general statements, but no "follow this how to do plan". I had to learn all of that the hard way. And now that I have all this knowledge from trial and error, I find myself being labeled and considered as a useless caretaker, even though almost six years of my life and service from love was given up when I could have and probably should have been doing other things. And the $32,000 I spent on rabbits sure would be helpful nowadays. But it is what it is.

I plan to create a webpage that provides rabbit care information that is lacking on other sites. I plan to provide the ideal "how to" plan on rabbit care that will link to all relevant articles on existing rabbit network pages. I plan to link to rabbit blogs that have a minimum of rabbit owners with limited single rabbit experiences who are the expert critics filled with general hateful remarks for other rabbit lovers who make innocent but regrettable mistakes due to a lack of knowledge. I want to provide a welcoming and positive model in contrast to the typical exclusionary and critical paradigm that I've found among overly protective, self-righteous and self-appointed rabbit experts. That's what's needed... more love and less disdain for people who make innocent mistakes.

As soon as I get back on my feet, I plan to adopt a bunny, kitty and doggie and raise them together to demonstrate the power of love. Well, so much for my rabbit plans. Best wishes and Happy Thanksgiving to all at Humane and Merry Christmas and Happy New Year! Good luck with your organizational and personal goals. And thanks again for everything! Let me know if I can ever be of service and I'll try my best.

Blake

Re: Grant Proposal

Heather
Dec 3, 2013

To

Blake Walker

Hi Blake,

I think you did a really good job on this proposal, especially considering, as you noted, that you didn't have a lot of background info on HUMANE. Thank you for doing this! Would be interested to know what prospective funders you might be able to identify for us - we've had funding from the Petco Foundation, and have submitted proposals to Oxbow's grant program and a few others (unsuccessfully) - a lot of the bigger funders focus on Cats and dogs exclusively, but it's been a while since I've researched anything so perhaps things have changed and/or there are new prospects now in existence.

Thank you!
Heather

P.S. A couple who adopted from us before, will be adopting Amber and Amberly!

Hi Heather,

Attached is the preliminary grant proposal to address your organization needs as explained to me during lunch with Cat. Please review it at your convenience and make any corrections you deem necessary. I created the proposal using PowerPoint to give you the additional flexibility of giving this proposal as a slide presentation to potential grantors or other audiences.

This proposal is missing a cover letter and signature page, but I can provide that should you decide to proceed with this effort. If you give me the green light, I will identify likely donors from grantor databases and forward that information to you. Subsequently, you could print the final hard copies and submit them to appropriate donors.

Good luck and Happy Thanksgiving!

Blake

Re: Grant Proposal

Blake Walker
Dec 4, 2013

To   heather@outlook.com

Hi Heather...

I'm glad to hear you have found Amberly and Amber a dependable forever home with loving parents. I was just thinking about them today and was going to ask you if you needed more room to accommodate other more desperate rabbits that I could take them back for a while since the weather is no longer hot. But of course finding a good forever home is the ultimate, and again I'm very grateful to you for doing that. Please let me know if you should ever hear about Ivory/Pinky, and Psycho/Pink. Has Galbani/Mustard gotten any adoption inquiries yet? Did one of your volunteers adopt BooBoo like they did NoNose?

I presume Brigit/Gorby continue to be healthy and loved. Both Brigit and Gorby had some health challenges that they fought to overcome, so just being healthy is a big deal for them. Between the two of them, I spent around $6,500 for veterinary care as both required multiple operations and months of medication. Brigit/Gorby are among the sweetest and most affectionate couples I've ever seen, after Amberly/Amber. In fact, all of my long-term bunnies had a lot of love in them, except for that wilder couple Psycho/Pink who were a bit hyperactive... so I'm very glad they're not longer stuck in an RV. I'm also glad Galbani and Mustard have made each other happy like in a story book dream. I can only be envious, lol.

I'm also glad to hear you are still interested in seeking additional funding sources. I know the proposal needs a lot of tweaking... the contents, once updated can also be cut and pasted into a document, grants template or RFP depending upon the submission format that is required by various organizations. That's one of the reasons I use PowerPoint as the preliminary format for its easy universal transferability and also as a potential slide presentation that can easily be modified with new slides in/out along with the ability to synch with other audio/visual formats and Internet links, when serving as a presentation template before groups or as an emailed presentation read only file.

As you are still interested in submitting funding proposals to various potential grantors, I will now conduct the research from different charitable funding databases, and also seek smaller grantors who would like more localized efforts and bang for their bucks. I don't think the larger animal rights groups and specialty care organizations would be much interested in rabbits without a full press concerted and labor intensive lobbying of their board members as their outreach programs tend to be general and overreaching, with high concentration on organizational PR and competitive national public fund raising, as I've noticed in my contacts with PETA and ASCPA.

The reality with large animal welfare organizations is they tend to be "black holes" where the sound of air sucking through a venturi is often evident. The reply from their staff to my inquiries has been the typical organizational PR bullshit where their main effort is to farm bleeding hearts into one of the many programs... primarily placing yet another anonymous soul into their fund raising data banks. And while PETA is more sympathetic to rabbits due to the highly publicized fur issues with celebrities, I'm disappointed they don't concentrate more pro-actively on rabbits since it appears much of domestic furs comes from skinning bunnies, often skinning them alive. While PETA uses horrific photos of abuse to animals, including rabbits, they seem to be focused on promoting rather than supporting, and both organizations rely on professional staff for their political lobbying and fund raising outreaches, with very little if anything returning to local community groups.

Funding for small local "hands on" rescue groups almost always is a local effort to seek and find funding sources often overlooked by larger animal relevant groups, particularly the nationals. I would suggest guerrilla tactics that include inroads to non-traditional forms of funding, where larger grants that will typically pass over small groups can instead be replaced by smaller donors among the charitable community. Of course the gold mine would be connecting to a network of celebrities... or at the least working through a list of B level celebs to reach the A level ones who have their own charities and could spare at least ten grand for pet causes that may be in some ways related to their programs.

For example, among my friends is a person who is active in MMA... but she has many connections to more popular celebs. I also have a friend who is an ex-employee of an A minus list publisher who still gets in the news periodically, who still has good contacts. We can explore potential donor contacts within your own organization by making lists of professionals and minor celebrities who may be persuaded to the support the cause of rabbit rescue and adoption. As you know, the value of celebrity participation is it draws attention among their fan base. I can draft a funding strategy that includes thinking out of the box in developing funding sources where on the surface, none may exist. In addition, standard donor lists will be examined to ascertain the appropriateness of their organizational or individual foundation missions to rabbit rescue efforts.

As I've just completed ghostwriting my uncle's memoirs of WWII, I have lots of time on my hands again as I'm taking a mental break from working on two other books in progress, so I have plenty of time to develop a fund raising program for you. Of course once I identify some sources, we will need to modify the funding proposal to different submission formats, at which time I will need to have access to more information about Humane, including:

List of administrators and contact information
List of board members and general info, including their professional titles
Humane's P&L for the past 3 years with budgetary summaries
Description of HUMANE's formalized programs
Detail of HUMANE's needs, and other current and historical accomplishments

When you get a chance, perhaps we should meet at local Starbucks to discuss some of these parameters after I have identified a dozen potential sources as part of a dual fund raising approach involving both institutional and non-traditional donor strategies. As the weather is cooling down, a nice hot cup of latte would help stimulate our thought processes... of course the coffee is on me if you provide the interest, open mind, and serious desire to explore, rather than to limit the possibilities. As you already know, fund raising is basically a persistence game like sales... lots of rejection, but each No is one step closer to the eventual YES. It's a numbers game where odds improve in direct relationship to quantity and quality of the fund raising program.

Now that you've let me know you're still interested in my assistance in your fund raising endeavors, I will make a serious effort to beat the bushes to see how many birds come flying out at us so we may capture some of them. I should have a list of potential donors and a funding strategic plan ready for you before Christmas. I'm hoping you all are doing fine and finding much emotional fulfillment in your rabbit rescue and personal activities. I trust you enjoyed family time during Thanksgiving and look forward to more holiday related shopping.... or maybe not, lol. This is the time of year when I usually become a hobbit and do more introspection than fraternization, to avoid the inevitable family drama.

Let's keep in touch and progress in our common passions... loving bunnies, lol.

Best wishes,

Blake

On Tuesday, December 3, 2013 8:34 PM, Heather wrote:
Hi Blake,

I think you did a really good job on this proposal, especially
considering, as you noted, that you didn't have a lot of background info
on HUMANE. Thank you for doing this! Would be interested to know what
prospective funders you might be able to identify for us - we've had
funding from the Petco Foundation, and have submitted proposals to Oxbow's
grant program and a few others (unsuccessfully) - a lot of the bigger
funders focus on Cats and dogs exclusively, but it's been a while since
I've researched anything so perhaps things have changed and/or there are
new prospects now in existence.

Thank you!
Heather

P.S. A couple who adopted from us before, will be adopting Amber and
Amberly!

Hi Heather,

Attached is the preliminary grant proposal to address your organization
needs as explained to me during lunch with Cat. Please review it at your
convenience and make any corrections you deem necessary. I created the
proposal using PowerPoint to give you the additional flexibility of giving
this proposal as a slide presentation to potential grantors or other
audiences.

This proposal is missing a cover letter and signature page, but I can
provide that should you decide to proceed with this effort. If you give
me the green light, I will identify likely donors from grantor databases
and forward that information to you. Subsequently, you could print the
final hard copies and submit them to appropriate donors.

Good luck and Happy Thanksgiving!

Blake

Grant proposals

    Blake Walker
    Dec 6, 2013

To

    heather@outlook.com
Hi Heather...

I have done preliminary research and have identified a dozen appropriate prospective funding sources, with another dozen that I'm currently exploring for appropriateness. Before I may continue to devote more time and effort into this project, I need you and/or Cat to review the attached Agreement for your discussion, negotiation, and approval. Once you have agreed to my services and to provide necessary information as requested by prospective donors, I will aggressively pursue the attainment of funds for Humane Rabbit Rescue.

Please let me know if you wish to discuss this proposed agreement. We can meet anytime at a Starbucks near you and Cat to develop an understanding and agreement on the scope, time line, and particulars of future funding proposals. I presume you are both busy with your rabbits, work, volunteers and the obligations of life like Christmas shopping, so I'm open to your convenience for scheduling a follow-up meeting.

I trust you'll enjoy your rabbit weekend, lol.

Best wishes,

Blake

This document contains the entire AGREEMENT between HUMANE RABBIT RESCUE
.doc
Download

Merry Christmas

Blake Walker
Dec 25, 2013

To

heather@outlook.com

Merry Christmas Heather,

I just wanted to let you know that you deserve all the gifts that you wrote on your "want list" to Santa for all the good that you've done for bunnies. Thanks again for sparing all of my bunnies the cruel fate of euthanasia at the animal shelters. I'm certain they're all having happier holidays than I could have given them, thanks to you.

Just wanted to let you know that I'm moving to Apple Valley with the new year. If you and Cat want me to pursue grant applications for Humane, we can do everything via email. If not, I hope your fund raising campaigns will continue to be successful so you will have the needed resources for the rabbits and reduce the financial impact on yourselves and Cat.

This message has been truncated

Happy New Year

The rabbit rescue people didn't follow-up on my grant proposal, where I was asking for a ten percent fee. I would continue to send greetings on holidays, hoping to get any type of a response... we're no longer interested in pursuing the route for a grant due to the low probability of success, or whatever. Instead, I received silence. Obviously, I was a rejected suitor, so after my Easter greetings, I stopped and for whatever reasons, Heather and Cat felt my offers of assistance weren't needed. It would have been nice to have received some acknowledgement, but I suppose like many employers, if they don't contact you after the job interview, they're just not interested. I suppose including Cat, the head of the rabbit group, at lunch to show my gratitude and proposals to volunteer and help in some capacity was a bust. I sensed Cat didn't like me for unknown reasons... it happens in job interviews all the time when interviewers for unknown reasons just don't like the interviewee. So be it. They don't need me, and I don't have any more rabbits to give up for adoption.

Fortunately, by the time I took them to lunch, it was two

months past the last day I ever saw my dear bunnies again so I was more composed and didn't show them that I was still feeling a hollow in my solar plexus from missing my rabbit children. After I got home from lunch, I had to get drunk to drown out some of my sorrows that discussing rabbits over lunch brought back to my emotional surface. I drank, looked at bunny pics and videos and cried myself to sleep before dinnertime. I kept wondering, when was this heartfelt feeling of loneliness going to disappear? I was still a bit choked up when I went shopping in the produce department that I had avoided for several months because every time I saw green leaf lettuce, celery or bananas, I would have this hollow pit in my chest feeling, as if my heart was still bleeding out my grief.

Finally, with the distractions of the Christmas and New Years season, I finally reached a point where I would not lament and cry over memories of my dear bunnies. I felt as if the emotional hurricane had finally passed enough where I could deal with the less intense tropical storm winds of sorrow with less emotional damage. I was determined to heal myself with the New Year. And I was going to do that without the needed support of family who didn't care, friends who didn't understand, my children who pretended everything was fine (except my daughter held a grudge for me missing her big wedding day in North Carolina, three thousand miles away because I was unable to find anyone to care for my rabbits –

thus I couldn't "give her away" to her husband), and the once compassionate rabbit rescue people who decided to shun me.

I would have to build my emotional strength up by myself. About that time, Comet Ison became a big deal on some pages of Face Book, and worrying about its trail impacting the Earth gave me some needed distractive focus. The comet was obliterated by its perigee around our sun, but my obsession with it helped me to forget my sorrows.

Chapter 7 – Emotional Triggers

A universal principle is normally operative in life that's called "action-reaction." This principle applies to just about everything we do in our daily lives. It affects how we feel about people and events, what we think about what happens in life, what we worry about, why we're happy or sad, and whether we slip into depression and despair. It appears there are certain "triggers" or events that seem to push people emotionally down that slippery emotional slope into deep and seemingly irretrievable depression.

In a weakened emotional state precipitated by a profound sense of loss (over people, things, events, etc.), people are at their greatest need for support that can take the form of compassion and empathy. Unfortunately, when depressed people do not receive adequate dosages of compassion and empathy, they can easily fall into the emotional traps of:

- self-pity
- neediness
- feeling of betrayal or abandonment
- prolonged loneliness
- debilitating emotional/mental illness
- self-destructive thoughts and behaviors
- incapacitation and total demotivation

Sometimes, all it takes to help a person from falling further into the depression pit is as simple as compassionate attention where someone close offers their hand, and pulls them out of their doldrums with supportive and distractive activities and conversation. The worse enemy of depression is being left alone to dwell on all that is wrong with life, and how life isn't fair because it dealt them a rotten deal when they deserved a good deal for being a good person.

Predators don't get depressed. Why? It's because they don't feel sorry for themselves because when they feel down, they get up and find their next victim. They satisfy their hunger for attention by focusing on activity that takes their minds away from sadness and depression. When they succeed in preying on someone, they feel satisfaction and elation from the adrenalin rush as part of "the hunt and kill."

People who are not predators, who are not adrenalin junkies, who are not self-directive, and who need emotional support from others are snared in an emotional trap of external dependency that cannot be resolved from within. When a person slides down the slippery slope of chronic depression, recurring thoughts of suicide are likely to occur. When I was at my lowest, I bought a set of samurai swords that included a tantō (knife) and wakizashi (short sword) used by samurais to commit ritual suicide, or seppuku, commonly known as hari kari. In case I chickened out due to the pain of stabbing oneself in the gut, I also bought a 40 caliber Glock.

What triggered me to contemplate suicide? I had been busy with caring for my rabbits for almost six years, and suddenly there was a huge void. I had too much time on my hand, was depressed, lonely, and had nothing to do, or anything I felt like doing. My only diversion was getting drunk daily on a six pack or more of beer, then falling sound asleep. My television was on almost 24/7 to provide me a constant background of noise and virtual human company. But I could not get motivated to get out of bed, except to use the toilet or to prepare food. I got to the point that I didn't feel like getting up to face another lonely depressive day (and the winter cold, rain and gloom didn't help as feeling secure and warm under my blankets felt much better than the frigid temperatures inside a motor home because I didn't run the furnace, and only used a small space heater).

On the very rare occasions that I would receive a call from my mother or son, I would keep the conversation short and decline any invitations to partake in any social functions. Over the 3 months that I grieved for my bunnies, I may have talked on the phone a total of 5 times. I came to prefer my solitude instead of having to make up answers to appear as if everything was alright, when it wasn't. But what was I to do, start crying and letting others know that I was depressed and didn't know how to get out of the web? I was too proud to cry in front of people who knew me, as I had always tackled my problems head on like a real man, not a wimp.

Chapter 8 – RECOVERY

Well, obviously I didn't commit suicide. I didn't even attempt suicide because I fortunately found enough excuses to stay alive… and I didn't want to fail at attempting suicide, just to become a brainless vegetable burden to my family and society. So my conclusion was to toss out that idea, and to reflect on the irrationality of my life at that point. I made lists of everything worth living for, and tried to describe my feeling of despair and worthlessness. I no longer felt I had a purpose for living, as I didn't have rabbits that depended on me for their very lives. My human children were grown, and my mother was living with my oldest sister. I had a few "drinking buddies" that rarely called, but would only want to hang out for drinking and womanizing. I no longer could afford to womanize, and I had lost interest in such a frustrating and unpredictable activity and I did all of my drinking in my RV to drown out my sorrows. I wouldn't be good company for anyone.

I decided to be more proactive, because I didn't like the feeling of despair that I felt trapped in. I looked on craigslist and found interviews for screen extras in Hollywood, so I called and made an appointment. During my private closed door interview, the casting agent asked me to read a script. Ironically, the script had a line about pets and my eyes watered up, and my voice cracked as I attempted to finish reading the audition script. Then I broke down and cried.

The casting agent felt sorry for me, and asked me what was going on inside. So I confessed that I thought I was already over the grief of giving up all my bunnies for adoption to a rabbit rescue group, and I felt lonely and purposeless. She smiled in a compassionate manner, and advised me, "You can have another bunny, but just have one and no more." I thanked her, wiped my eyes dry, and looking down at the ground to avert eye contact with an entire room of serious actors and actresses waiting for their interviews, then walked as quickly away as I could, never to attempt another screen extra audition.

When I got home, I couldn't believe that I lost it like I did at the audition. I felt ashamed and unmanly. I felt like a wimp. But fortunately, no one else had to know so I never mentioned it to anyone else... it would be my little secret until now. I figured I was still too emotionally weak to interact with people, so I reverted to drinking beer and watching television. I found myself watching lots of television news... I knew the news broadcast schedule for every day of the week... during the weekdays, there was news on at least one broadcast channel every hour of the day from 4AM through 11:30PM, and I often watched other people's misery, calamities, and Catastrophes played out before my eyes. Though I was emotionally removed from the terrible news stories, I thought to myself, "golly, I'm sure glad that's not happening to me!"

In a pathetic and twisted sort of way, by watching other people's bad news, I didn't feel my situation was nearly as sad, and the daily news had a comparative Cathartic effect that stopped me from feeling sorry for myself. It was ironic that the bad things that happened to others on a daily basis actually made me feel more fortunate about my own life. I began to count my blessings that while I was no longer employed due to a recession lay off, I had monthly income from the state unemployment program that was extended by the federal government thanks to President Obama.

Though I no longer lived in a house because my mother sold it when the real estate market tanked as a strategy to push me and my rabbits out of her house, I had bought a used RV and I was not homeless on the streets. I was secure in my own space, had AC going on, a refrigerator, microwave, television, computer, Internet, a car, landline and cell phone, and some very nice neighbors and the park manager who I would go shoot pool with from time to time. My ex-girlfriend would visit and stay over from time to time, but left after I got drunk and we argued as usual. I really didn't have it that bad, except I missed my rabbit children a hell of a lot.

I started to see the glass as half full, instead of half empty with a crack where water would seep out, with the bottom in sight. I started to think about things more objectively and what lessons my emotional journey with my dear bunnies had taught me.

When I started to write about all the life lessons I had directly or indirectly gleaned from my dedicated care for my bunnies, observing their interactions, becoming part of their tribe, and watching many lives start and end, I came to some conclusions that helped me to take a more realistic attitude about life, and how I was going to tackle it in the future.

Lessons about life:

- It is fragile. One moment you are alive, the next you are dead. One moment you have consciousness, feeling, sensing and thinking – the next you are unconscious, brain-dead, and a slab of dead meat like any animal.
- Life is impartial – it does not demand that one live to one's full potential (whatever that is), nor sets values on behavior, self-image or morality. These are all societal values and conditions. Life is surviving – living in the moment without guarantee of the next moment. People do whatever they feel compelled to do to survive – to live.
- Life has no intrinsic value, except that it separates animate objects from inanimate objects. Living entities express themselves in various ways, particularly through movement and destruction of other life forms to support the viability of their own lives. In the overall

scheme of Earth, the solar system and the universe, living things – particularly humans – are not significant nor requirement for continuity of the planet. Living things are more like parasites as they contribute little to nothing to support the ecosystem and in many respects act to destroy the natural environment.

- The only value to life is what we make it – what our belief systems are that result from socialization, acculturation, religious beliefs, brainwashing and desire for carnal pleasures, creature comforts and materialism.
- No two lives are alike – not only genetically, stimulus-response, feelings, decision-making, beliefs and the responses to daily situations with resultant positive or negative learning experiences.
- One's life is of private value to oneself, as no other persons can imagine or emotively appreciate the nuances unique to each individual. No others can really care more for a person than they must care for themselves.
- Life is a series of trips, loosely connected into a journey of experiences. The quality of the trips determine in large part the level of satisfaction and desire to seek more from life – or to become cynical in suffering its endurance. Some people become zombies – the walking dead.

- Modern humans in developed nations are pushed by social standards to rush and be efficient producers – just to get to nowhere. Then society calls that living and building on one's goals, aspirations and dreams. BS.

Lessons about illnesses and injuries:

- It usually happens without warning then symptoms suddenly get very bad within a day
- Its level of severity determines the level of debility or disability.
- Recovery extent and rehabilitation period depends on person's immunity response
- In hind site, the majority of incidents could have been prevented through precaution and caution.
- What doesn't kill you does not make one stronger, except one builds temporary immunities after overcoming particular diseases. Injuries are usually with life-long consequences and weaken the areas injured. It can also wear you down in the long run if your recuperative powers fade with age and declining body/mental conditioning.
- Situations and events that have made me stronger (or has been wearing me down?)

1. A thousand scratches, nicks, cuts and bruises from caring for the rabbits in the rabbitat from fencing
2. Daily dirt in finger nails, cuts and scratches
3. Bumping head, dropping objects, splashing bacteria on to eyes
4. Extreme temperatures >100 or <40 degrees outside when feeding rabbits
5. Being awaken by rabbits early in morning
6. Listening for attacks by Cat on rabbitat fencing several times each night
7. Climbing bar stool and balancing several times day/night to check on rabbits
8. Inhaling rabbit fur when sweeping or vacuuming
9. Touching rabbit poop several times each day
10. Bitten several times by rabbit
11. Cutting 200 strokes each day preparing rabbit food
12. Feeling compassion and empathy for rabbits emotional and physical disposition
13. Exposure to Pasturella and other soil and rabbit borne bacteria
14. Being repeatedly insulted, berated and verbally abused by ex-girlfriend

15. Listening to daily ravings of a mad person with anti-social views (racist, sexist, classist, anti-humanity, paranoia, braggadocios, and narcissism, etc.)

16. Constantly dropping things, banging into objects, getting nicked and bruised.

- People who rarely get sick or injured tend to have stronger genetic make up to start with. Consequently, they are better able to tackle the uncertain environmental challenges that come their way. However, even the most physically and emotionally fit individuals could still succumb to a deadly spider bite, or have a life threatening mishap such as a simple slip and fall.

- Accidents are constantly waiting to happen in an instant of inattention or from random exposure to unseen toxins, bacteria, mold, insects, cuts, nicks, contaminated water splash back, dropping things, getting burns and bites. It seems like everyday some unexpected accident happens

So, how do we overcome sadness, sorrow, despair and hopelessness? Besides comparing our own misery to those who have it much worse, thinking on life lessons and why life is valuable and worth living despite all of its disappointments, what steps can be taken to free oneself from the chains of insidious depression?

It's not as simple as positive thinking inside a vacuum tube. Let's take a look at each cause of sadness, sorrow, despair and hopelessness and propose real world workable solutions for each type of situation that people have successfully used to overcome and survive hopelessness.

Failure in relationships, career	1
Rejection and/or replacement by significant partner	2
Financial ruination	3
Debilitating Illnesses or injuries	4
Loss of loved ones	5
Catastrophic material losses	6
No way out of misery	7
Long term excruciating pain	8
Emotional pain and suffering	9
Physical pain and suffering	10
Loneliness leading to despondency	
Sudden poverty and/or homelessness	11
Profound emotional disappointments	12
Cumulative unresolved major problems	13
Total helplessness, real or perceived	14
Fear induced severe anxiety of future	15
Unattainable Social expectations	16
Injustice without relief	17
Keeping long term secrets of wrong doings	18
Sustained fear of discovery for wrong doings	18
Lost of personal independence	20
Moral hypocrisy causing sustained cognitive dissonance	21
Legal or government persecution and/or prosecution	22
Unfulfilled dreams and goals	23
Negative worldview and philosophical perspectives	24

Remember the happy person described at the beginning of this book? Why was that person able to be happy and content while others allow themselves or even drive themselves to become straddled with sadness, sorrow, despair and hopelessness? Let's look at a strategy of awareness that, like alcoholic anonymous, can help to overcome depression and despair.

Stages of overcoming sadness, sorrow, despair and hopelessness

The 7 "A's"

Acknowledgement

Admission

Acceptance

Anxiety

Activity

Antithesis

Actualization

Let's discuss each of the 7 "A's" to ascertain how self-help can be an effective method to self-healing. After all, you can lead a horse to the water, but you can't force it to drink, right?

Acknowledgement – If a person is in a state of denial that a serious problem exist, then they will not bother to take steps to resolve it. Self-honest is tantamount and a precondition to finding the best strategy to solve whatever personal problems that might exist or are impacted by a particular condition. The first step is acknowledgement that a problem "might" exist, and that others have experienced such problems.

Admission – The next step takes an honesty for people to admit to their problems, weaknesses, needs, and problems. The problem of perhaps well-intentioned people criticizing only acts to make people more defensive and to deny their state of affairs. It would be far more supportive for people not to label someone, such as, "You're an alcoholic, or drug addict, or sex pervert or emotionally ill or too depressed." The problem with external criticism and name calling is it tends to be counterproductive because it makes the persons suffering from various afflictions to clam up and feel defensive, thus they pretend they are actually normal – that nothing's wrong. Sometimes, honest hurts, so people will deny the truth.

Acceptance – Admitting a condition exist is a start, but accepting it is essential to internalizing and realizing that action must be taken, and the person responsible to resolve one's problems is not external, but primarily an internal one. Others can help, but the only one who can solve it is oneself.

Anxiety – Once a person accepts their true condition, doing nothing about it causes the feeling of constructive anxiety, or a subconscious nervousness and motivation to do something about it... to take action to solve the dilemma. When people are comfortable with their condition, they tend to do nothing but to maintain the status quo. After all, "if it ain't broke, why fix it?" Anxiety serves the purpose of causing people to act to reduce and eliminate the uncomfortable feeling of anxiety.

Activity – Doing nothing to solve one's problems is based on the failure to accomplish the previous steps of awareness. However, once a person is fully aware of their situation, they will instinctively seek solutions through activities that focus on reducing anxiety and emotional discord. This is an ideal time for engaging others to lend a supportive hand, because the motivation to find effective solutions encourages helpers and seekers to feel empowered by positive step by step results.

Antithesis – Oftentimes, the solutions to personal problems is as simple as doing the opposite of what go an person into their dilemmas in the first place. For example, people who become obese need to do the opposite of what made them obese... simply eat much less than what is craved. People who become depressed due to various events or people may simply need to avoid certain people and situations to give them the needed time to recover, strengthen their emotions and to take necessary effective actions.

Actualization – When a person reaches the solution step and succeeds, it's a testament to the realization of every previous step, from acknowledgment through antithesis to reach an actual solution and problem resolution.

Chapter 9 – Prevention

As in physical medicine, emotional states respond to similar strategies. How many times have we heard that "an ounce of prevention is worth a pound of cure?" It's an age old adage for a reason… it really works! Attitude is instrumental in preventing emotional turmoil that can lead to depression and hopelessness. And the doorway to attitude is founded in the mind… thoughts based on perspectives and values that people have adopted from society and life experiences. One of the surest way to combat depression creep, or the sudden voids and vacancies caused by significant or Catastrophic losses, is the formation of a belief system that accurately places our lives into its realistic relationship to others in society. Wisdom is the result of tried and true strategies and tactics to deal with all that life throws our way, the obstacle courses, challenges, games, and how far we get along the course, and whether we end up feeling like a winner or loser.

Wisdom isn't universal, but defines a set of skills, attitudes, perspectives and methods to get through the unpredictable obstacle courses in life that works in specific situations. Therefore a different set of wisdom may be needed when faced with different challenges, particularly new extreme situations that one has never faced before. Wisdom is having the faith in oneself that somehow, you'll get through the course with your feet under you, your head and heart intact. Subjective wisdom isn't all it's made up to be, when it sounds like a bunch of excuses

A buddy forwarded an email with wise advice from a 90 year old lady who wrote a column for a small town newspaper. Upon reading these jewels of wisdom, it occurred that they're all methods to acquiesce to life for people who felt little control or took few risks to really experience the breath and depth of life.

Following are the presumptive experientially based wisdom by Regina Brett, 90 years old, of the Plain Dealer, Cleveland , Ohio .... "To celebrate growing older, I once wrote the 45 lessons life taught me. It is the most requested column I've ever written. My odometer rolled over to 90 in August, so here is the column once more."

My responses follow each pearl of wisdom, as bullet points... some replies are meant to be obviously "tongue in cheek."

1. Life isn't fair, but it's still good.
   - Sometimes.
2. When in doubt, just take the next small step.
   - Sometimes better to observe and wait things out.
3. Life is too short – enjoy it.
   - At least you can try.
4. Your job won't take care of you when you are sick your friends and family will.
   - I'd rather depend on a good health plan.
5. Pay off your credit cards every month.
   - Better to rely on a debit card to eliminate debt.
6. You don't have to win every argument. Stay true to yourself.
   - Better to say to people, "You have your opinions, and I have mine... is that okay with you? If not, then go fuck yourself, asshole."
7. Cry with someone. It's more healing than crying alone.
   - You never want to have anyone see you cry because they will always think you're a weak wimp.
8. It's OK to get angry with God. He can take it.
   - God is fake... the Annunakis are real
9. Save for retirement starting with your first paycheck.
   - Enjoy your money while you're young and have good health... there's social security, senior housing, food stamps, free healthcare, senior centers, and free cell phone for you when you get old and slow.

10. When it comes to chocolate, resistance is futile.
    - So is beer and sex... but when you're real old, only beer will matter.
11. Make peace with your past so it won't screw up the present.
    - Some things you just can't let go of, until you take revenge... let's be real about this. It's only when revenge is impossible that you can let it go.
12. It's OK to let your children see you cry.
    - Absolutely NOT! They will lose respect for you
13. Don't compare your life to others. You have no idea what their journey is all about.
    - Who cares about other people's journey anyway? Only your *true loyal* friends matter, especially when blood relatives may criticize and shun you.
14. If a relationship has to be a secret, you shouldn't do it.
    - Bullshit big time. You should be able to fuck who you want if you can get away with it, as long as the old lady doesn't find out and throw a cow, hahah.
15. Everything can change in the blink of an eye, but don't worry, God never blinks.
    - God sucks and will let you down at the worse possible moments, and then it's up to you to get your ass off the ground and back on your feet cuz most likely no one will give a shit, and they'll all try to avoid you.

16. Take a deep breath. It calms the mind.
    - But first, you gotta load the bong with medical cannabis.
17. Get rid of anything that isn't useful. Clutter weighs you down in many ways.
    - Toss out books you're likely never to read, cuz all the recent stuff is on the web. Get rid of useless relationships that only suck off your time, money, energy, positive attitude, and creativity by burdening you with all their baggage and emotional issues.
18. Whatever doesn't kill you really does make you stronger.
    - I like the old banged up car analogy better... it just means you made it through another jump, but now your suspension is fucked up and you vibrate when going down the road... so you're not dead, but sometimes it looks and feels worse than death.
19. It's never too late to be happy. But it's all up to you and no one else.
    - When you're around happy people who like you and enjoy your company, you will likely feel happy too. But if you're around shitty user needy fucks, then you'll be miserable like them.

20. When it comes to going after what you love in life, don't take no for an answer.
    - It all depends if you can afford the cost of admission, or the bouncer or cops will slam your ass to the ground.
21. Burn the candles, use the nice sheets, and wear the fancy lingerie. Don't save it for a special occasion. Today is special.
    - Good looking women with tight bodies look better naked... the not so good looking ones need to put on illusions like make-up, fancy lingerie and perfume.
22. Over prepare, then go with the flow.
    - If you're gunna go with the flow anyway, why bother to prepare? How about all the super hero patriots in our military who over prepare, just to have their transport choppers downed by a jihadist rag head's RPG? Those jihadist camel jockeys don't even wear Kevlar armor and helmets and don't fly planes, drones or choppers, and we're still getting our asses kicked in them god-forsaken mud huts villages.
23. Be eccentric now. Don't wait for old age to wear purple.
    - When you're young and eccentric, people think you're weird or a psycho, but when you're old, people expect you to be eccentric, so it's cool.

24. The most important sex organ is the brain.
    - Bullshit... it's the size of your hard cock... ask Gary, cuz he knows, lol
25. No one is in charge of your happiness but you.
    - True, but lots of people will try to fuck that up for you.
26. Frame every so-called disaster with these words 'In five years, will this matter?'
    - Hell yeah, you might become a jihadist cripple with astronomical medical bills that you can't pay, then you suffer and die.
27. Always choose life.
    - Sometimes, life isn't what it's made up to be, and it's better to commit suicide after you kill off your enemies, lol. Or die trying. No surrender, no retreat.
28. Forgive.
    - But only if they deserve it... if not, don't every trust them again, and given an opportunity, give them back a taste of their own medicine... but don't go out of you way to do that, unless it was serious and you really hate them and are losing sleep over it, lol.
29. What other people think of you is none of your business.
    - Bullshit, because what they think will limit your opportunities in life or in getting prime pussy!

30. Time heals almost everything. Give time more time.

  - No, time heals only minor physical and emotional wounds. The serious ones need medical or psychiatric treatment, otherwise you become a murderous psycho like Elliott Rodger, the Isla Vista/UCSB serial killer.

31. However good or bad a situation is, it will change.

  - But it could get much worse, so maybe you'd be lucky if it didn't change too much too soon.

32. Don't take yourself so seriously. No one else does.

  - D'oh... is that why people get shot from road rage or "mad dogging"... or over someone else's bitch or a jihadist pool game?

33. Believe in miracles.

  - For starters, there really is a Santa Claus, tooth fairy, and money grows on trees... and every pretty gal wants to suck your dick. Yeah, right.

34. God loves you because of who he is, not due to anything you did or didn't do.

  - Anyone who can read the Bible *literally* will notice that god tells us he's a jealous god who demands blind obedience, love and worship... and if you don't give that to him, he kills you, your entire family, and the whole jihadist town you lived in. Read the goddamn Bible and stop putting your own jihadist retarded interpretation. God hates mankind and plans to return at the end of time to kill everyone except the 144,000 kiss asses that he has already chosen from his bloodline.

35. Don't audit life. Show up and make the most of it now.

- If you don't audit, you won't know how much money you have, who is cheating you, and you'll become just another chump, sucker! This is especially true for relationships filled with users and gold diggers.

36. Growing old beats the alternative of dying young.

- I'd rather die young while setting a new land speed world record than growing old, decrepit, stupid, and relying on others to change my diapers.

37. Your children get only one childhood.

- Then they grow up and become ungrateful assholes like mine.

38. All that truly matters in the end is that you loved.

- Then you realize how your wasted your life loving others and trying to make them happy while sacrificing your own personal pursuit of happiness, and they ended up disliking you for not doing more for them.

39. Get outside every day. Miracles are waiting everywhere.
    - However, it's likely you'll never find one... unless you win the lottery or Kate Upton thinks you're hot... both of which will never happen.
40. If we all threw our problems in a pile and saw everyone else's, we'd grab ours back.
    - No... We'd pour gasoline on it and toss in a match.
41. Envy is a waste of time. Accept what you already have, not what you need.
    - A poor person who doesn't envy the rich doesn't understand inequality of the rigged system, and will not take the necessary action to get themselves out of the gutter.
42. The best is yet to come...
    - Let's think about this... you're 90 years old and haven't accomplished much in your lifetime... hmmm, what can be better?
43. No matter how you feel, get up, dress up and show up.
    - Has anyone heard of staying in bed to enjoy the "afterglow" of good sex... or resting after an "all nighter"? WTF?

44. Yield.
   - Only if there's a stoplight or stop sign, otherwise, keep on trucking, or you may miss out. The world belongs to those who grab the bull by its horns, take risks, pushes others out of their way, and is willing to stand tall.
45. Life isn't tied with a bow, but it's still a gift."
   - No, life is the consequence of horny parents who made jihadist mistakes by not using birth control.
46. The challenge: It's estimated 93% won't forward this email.
   - Of course not, because this is like the stupidest advice I've ever read, bar none, the 7% who believed all this crappy "wisdom", you should forward this to their friends and family so they will know why you've been a loser. Real friends won't mind and won't judge you, but family will likely criticize, lol.

In response to these useless fake pearls of wisdom, I replied with some of my experiential wisdom gleaned from my mistakes in life and what seemed like a lifetime raising my bunnies.

- Respect others and never intentionally harm anyone.
- Be honest, but not through insulting presumptive accusations and opinions.
- Take the freedom to be who you are, as long as you don't intentionally cause harm to others.
- Accept and tolerate others, for better or for worse. You can't change them.
- Avoid dramatic and/or violent people.
- Keep things simple, stress free and drama free.
- Avoid people who don't like you, lie or deceive.
- Occasionally be around people who like you, or be alone.
- Give people respect until they prove they don't deserve it.
- Be as free as society permits, even when going against social norms.
- Don't buy into most cultural, religious and social norms and values... it's mostly
- bullshit if it doesn't pass the test of common practical sense or scientific facts.
- Accept full responsibility for your own actions or inaction, cuz no one else will.
- Treat others as they treat you, for better or worse. That's called justice.

- Avoid helping needy users who are ungrateful and will likely backstab you.
- Don't seek validation from others, and avoid their control mind games.
- Be upfront and without deceptive hidden agendas.
- Don't judge a book by its cover: in general, don't judge until after an experience.
- Accept it when you find you're wrong and learn from it to avoid doing it again.
- Don't look for credit or ego-centered validation, but know thyself honestly.
- Money is nice for its functional use and for no other reason that's useful.
- Be thankful for what you have and don't be greedy by exploiting others.
- Elderly people should know that a facelift doesn't make them young again.
- Do things that interest you, or give you fun or fulfillment, otherwise don't.
- Resist being mind fucked and manipulated by others for their own benefit.
- Avoid criminals and cops... they spell danger.
- Avoid commitments you can't keep or afford.
- Don't bother to impress anyone because in the end, it's all bullshit.

- Don't feel too badly about anything because it's mostly bullshit anyway.
- Avoid guilt trippers who use it to try to get something from you.
- It's okay not to be ambitious as long as you can survive without hurting others.
- Help others if it's worthwhile and not just another rip off from ungrateful users.
- When your time is up, take death by standing tall and not on you knees or flat on your back. Kill yourself before you end up in an ICU with needles everywhere, and you die without dignity like a soggy vegetable.

After my so-called friend received my responses, he changed his phone number and deleted his email address. I never bothered to drive to his house 30 miles away to visit him unannounced because I felt that if he wanted to remain friends, he would make an effort. If he didn't, then I didn't lose anyone besides someone who wasn't real and really didn't want to be my friend. Were I still in my depressed and self-pitying state, I might have become hurt and sad, but in my invigorated and self-confident state that resulted from soul searching, I decided the loss of his friendship was the shedding of unnecessary baggage, and that would make my trip through life much lighter in the future. I thought about the basic life questions, and derived answers that have been my shield against depression.

Answers to life's basic questions:

(1)   *What is life really all about?*
(2)   *Why are we here?*
(3)   *Do we have a purpose to fulfill in life?*
(4)   *How are we connected to each other?*
(5)   *Who Am I?*
(6)   *What's my relationship to others?*

1.   *What is life really about?*

- Life is about living and surviving while feeling and being alive versus being dead and inanimate
- Experiencing moment by moment as it unfolds – not denying, rejection or delusional
- Being appreciative of life itself as a transformative learning proposition if open to experiencing it
- Taking the time to feel alive and not in a hurry to get through it
- Allowing oneself to have honest feelings and emotions and to let them happen

- To feel life in its entirety, richness and depth – to laugh and cry, to hope and fear, to love and hate, to know, doubt and wonder as part of life's canvass
- To respect life in every form as a transformation of energy and consciousness from plants to animals, insects, bacteria to humans – all on the spectrum of life seeking to express and seek survival
- To accept death, to feel sadness and grief without knowing the transformation

2. *Why are we here?*
- We are here by random chance or choice of our parents or simply as a consequence of random sexual urges caused by hormonal instinct
- No matter where we go, there we are – whether by decision or by chance
- Circumstances, situations, opportunities and decisions have consequences and outcomes that are often unforeseen, unpredictable, uncertain and unknown
- To be free to be and express our true individuality and uniqueness
- To discover ourselves for who we really are – not simply products of social conditioning, peer and/or parental pressure and values or social/cultural/media norms

3.   *Do we have a purpose to fulfill in life?*

- The purpose in life is basically to survive to be free from pain, hunger, disease, suffering, and fear as much as one's natural constitution and financial situation will allow
- Each individual defines their own purpose(s) – some are simple, others are complex and multivariate depending upon circumstances, while some have no purpose whatsoever besides basic animal urges
- People tend to have certain general universal cultural tendencies for greed, hoarding, materialism, seeking the validation of others, seeking respect, wanting to control others, selfishness, deception and hidden motives etc. but the bottom line is the pursuit of self-benefiting advantages
- For many, life is simply a journey of discovery, learning and experiences with no greater plan or goal except to embrace all that life presents

4.   *How are we connected to each other?*

- We are all connected through societies that are responsive to the manipulations of leaders and popularly admired value and trend setters of social norms
- By the bio-electrical energy that is harnessed to keep us alive and conscious

- All energy is conserved as the spark of life upon the beginning and the end of life is transformed from and returned to the earth's ecological system as part of the universe
- Biological or non-biological receptors of energy area all related on the atomic level as energy and matter transformations into different states of each or both
- Our intellectual consciousness is no more than another level of awareness permitted by electrical impulses that interpret the internal and external environment into patterns of thought that include discrimination, association, cause-effect, assimilation, segregation, Categorization, organization, generalization, symmetry, inclusion, exclusion, rejection, and etc.
- Our emotional consciousness is more primal and basically responds to innate genetic survival instincts and predispositions such as fear, aggression, affection, flight or fight impulse, curiosity, discovery, learning, affinity, preference, discrimination, hate, love, prejudice, greed, insecurity and etc.

5. *Who Am I?*
- I know who I am, but what are you? I am the combined product of genetic inheritance –DNA that gives me functional abilities and propensities and the cybernetic feed back learning loop mostly from trial and error that

results from interacting with the environment from a self-benefiting/self-perpetualizing

- perspective in order to minimize negative consequences while seeking to fulfill and experience positive outcomes
- As such, in general I attribute who I am and who/what I am and have become to the aggregate interaction of my genetic make-up and reaction to my life experiences and people of personal consequence:
- 20% DNA's genetic potential and limitations
- 10% parental influences – mostly modeling and subconscious
- 10% society and peer norms of self-worth and social validation
- 10% random chance situations and opportunities
- 50% personal decisions for better or worse, progress or destruction

6.   *What's my relationship to others?*
- I am not the roles that I feel compelled to play in society in order to survive and earn a paycheck from people who occupy positions of control or regulate the economic system – though elements of who I am is expressed in situational decisions according to my social, intellectual, emotional, mental, creative and physical skills as appropriate.

- ·Half of who I am is what I have come to accept and the other half is who I want to become, wish I could be, my hopes and dreams all in a nutshell. As I age, I find that I must accept more of what I have become as reality
- My relationships in life with others is primarily to satisfy instinctive genetic social and emotional needs that may likely exist to varying degrees as modified by emotional reactions to social and philosophical experiences
- I exist independently of others as a separate unique individual
- In so far as we live by choice and circumstance as part of a larger society, social engagement of various types are inevitable
- ·Whereas forced social contact and conditioning occur through government and parental mandates such as compulsory schooling and family environment, once freed of those constraints I am free to choose my associations as I may desire according to my personal needs whether based upon emotional, mental, physical, intellectual, recreational, escapist, spiritual or other needs
- Where I am able to choose my social interactions both in private and public settings, I seek to fulfill my hierarchical Maslovian needs as an aware and

self-actualized person with consideration for safety/security, basic survival needs and other unfulfilled needs and desires

- As a separate individual, I may choose to minimize my exposure and contact to others by living a reclusive lifestyle or I may choose to be a social gadfly or any level of social engagement in between

- In general I prefer minimal contact and interaction with people to avoid the high probability of eventual conflict, misunderstandings, competition, deception, ungraciousness, exploitation, drama, stupidity, disappointment, etc.

- I prefer to interact with others on the level of philosophical discourse and political discussion in a truth-seeking paradigm devoid of egotism and personal attacks for differences in opinion or analyses. I seek to separate fact from fiction in the real world of multi-layered deception and parasitic relationships with distorted social roles required to support the social and cultural hierarchical structure defined by overt and covert subtle forms of racism, sexism, ageism, intellectualism, classicism and etc.

Lessons about death:

- People grieve the lost of loved ones for many reasons – lost of companionship, lost of love, lost of personal interaction, lost of money, lost of enjoyment, etc. But they adjust and in most cases, their memories are short and their days are also numbered so they move on to forget.
- Philosophically and emotionally, death of a loved one or pet confirms how fragile life itself really is – and how all that one is can be erased in a moment of suffering
- People who suffer terminal diseases should have the option to have a humane way to die. Death is sometimes the best option to extreme suffering.
- All of your problems, worries, concerns, goals, dreams, aspirations, hopes, potential and relationships cease upon death – and it doesn't seem to matter much to anyone else.
- We all expect to die someday – but most want to put it off because they are fearful of what lies ahead after death, or they want more time to do those things they haven't succeeded in doing... but have convinced themselves that they could accomplish those things with more time. The reality is, they probably never will do most of the things they had desired or envisioned, even with added years.

- When you're dead, you're dead. You become just a body – an inanimate object.
- Sometimes, going through the trials and tribulations of living can feel worse than death – because in death there is peace and final relief.
- I feel sad and badly anytime one of our rabbits die because in retrospect I supposed in many instances it could have been prevented by closer attention, improved environment, and medical treatment. It feels like the lost of a close friend... forever.
- Having had a half dozen rabbits die in my hands/arms – it's a sharp contrast that one moment they are mobile and living and in the next instance they take their last breath and become lifeless and limp – non responsive.
- Under certain circumstances, death may be a welcome departure to life if it is filled with suffering, pain, unrelentless emotional or physical torture, destitute without any semblance of hope, and profound unhappiness with ones circumstances that can not be changed by oneself – for example being incarcerated or in a concentration camp.
- Likely many of my rabbits won't live past 5 years – will die before my lifespan is over
- I need to view rabbits as having shorter life span and likely to die of natural causes like Pasteurella, stasis, or other illnesses – diarrhea or accidents

- Living a fulfilling but shorter life is more meaningful and valuable than living a useless and purposeless long life
- Death appears to alleviate fear and other life anxieties
- Electrical energy impulses organized as stimulus response in cells differentiate living from inanimate objects so death is the cessation of the bio-electrical process
- Watching and expecting my rabbits to die early from Pasteurella makes me feel helpless – all I can do is to comfort them, give them proper care and affection.
- Giving unconditional love to animals is the same as giving to humans and the loss is equally missed
- Death is not a moral judgment – that it is bad and life is good.
- Death is a natural consequence of life as part of a natural cycle of birth to death
- Death occurs when all of the criteria necessary to sustain life is inadequate or missing
- Death is inevitable – it's not a matter of "if" but rather of "when" that is unpredictable under natural circumstances
- When a living creature dies, its physical aspects remain intact however the electrical pulses cease and consciousness disappears from the current reality.

- We feel justified to take another's life if we feel our life or that of a loved one is genuinely threatened with death or serious harm that could lead to death
- We feel it's okay to kill creatures for food, even though they are sentient
- We feel that needless killing and death is immoral and unjustifiable
- Sometimes death of individuals is a necessary sacrifice for the common survival
- Rulers want the death and sacrifice of the commons to preserve the elites
- When humans get wiped out by the Annunakis, the meek rabbits will inherit the earth and become the dominant species

Lessons about the soul:

- If humans have souls, then all life must also have souls as it is not evident that any life is elevated above another – either something is alive or it is inanimate.

- If there is no such thing as a soul, beyond people's fear of death and the need to validate one selves beyond this worldly existence, then it's foolish to invent something delusional that misplaces people's effort to live this life to its fullest – or to whatever degree people would otherwise feel compelled or complacent based on the belief the soul does not exist.

- How do we explain that more people now exist than has ever died? So where do all the new souls come from? Hindus explain that animals become human and vice versa so that means more animals have become humans than have been recycled back to animals.

- It appears that the difference between living things and inanimate objects is the manner by which energy is expressed and/or transformed into dynamic biological cells that enable motion.

- It is possible that the energy itself is the life force or soul that transcends and transforms from the physical receptacle(s) but is not destroyed due to Newton's Third Law of Thermodynamics – the conservation of energy.

- When a live entity is in direct contact with a dying entity and at the moment of death, the soul from the now dead entity passes into the living entity until it dissipates.

Lessons about God and gods:

- The probability exist that in the 12-15 billion years of the known universe that intelligent life far beyond that attained by Earth's 5 billion years does exist.

- It is possible these advanced life forms have technologies well beyond that attained by humans.

- It is possible the reference to gods by ancient human civilizations and cave paintings depict superior life forms that have been on Earth, and may have intervened in the development of humans from existing terrestrial life forms – such as implanting DNA into apes to create mankind.

- The monotheistic God depicted in the Bible, Koran and Torah is an angry, jealous, unforgiving, demanding, violent mass murderer... maybe the giant lizard like Annunaki gods referred in the Sumerian and Babylonian creation mythologies

- People created the notion of gods and eventually a singular God to try to sooth their superstitious need to feel safer faced with natural disasters. They created rituals to seek the favor of gods/God to spare them suffering and to permit them plentiful food supplies for survival from year to year. In fact, natural forces have existed and will continue to exist regardless of what people's religious beliefs or preferences may be.

- It is also possible that the Annunaki and their earthly descendants created religion to keep people in the bondage of fear and the belief that god is benevolent when in fact the race of Annunakis are conquerors and mass killers

- When another life extinction size meteor strikes the Earth in the unforeseeable future, no God will be there to spare human life – or any life that would be unable to survive the heat blast, debris, and years of winter.

- The Bible, science, genetics, Darwinism, the Mayan calendar and Sumerian religion all tie together to tell the entire picture of the creation of humans by the Annunaki "gods" and the prophesized end of human rule on earth.

- Anu is the leader & ruler of the Annunakis on Nibiru

- Satan or Lucifer is the leader & ruler of the Annunakis on earth who comprise one-third of the Annunakis who rebelled against Anu on their mother ship 7,200 years ago and were left on earth

- Satan is preparing to fight Anu when Nibiru returns

- Christ is the son of "god" – Anu whose DNA sperm was implanted into Mary

Lessons about happiness:

- Happiness is a state of mind – an internal emotion caused by the release of certain brain chemicals.
- The trigger of the release of happiness brain chemicals varies from person to person, but non-drug triggers include accomplishment, satisfaction of various material and ego needs, feeling of belonging, acceptance or love.
- Not everyone is capable of feeling happiness, and people feel intensity to varying degrees. The genetic brain programming and brain chemicals determine the duration, intensity and sensation of happiness.
- Serenity and peace of mind is one of the tenets of self-fulfillment and happiness as it places a person's state of mind back to its primordial natural state devoid of social and cultural norms that function to control and regulate beliefs and behaviors.
- Happiness is really an state of "mind over matter" – if a person doesn't mind the otherwise small and sometimes large irritants of life (inconvenience, disappointment, toxic relationships, bad luck, pain and injuries, etc.) – then it doesn't matter. This allows people to focus more on things that matter or really

should matter in the overall perspective of life as a protracted long-term proposition rather than a momentary or day by day paradigm.

- Non-judgmental attitude
- Accept circumstances and seek some benefit from all situations
- Don't dwell on the negatives and disappointments
- Minimize expectations of things controlled by others
- Focus on positive aspects of situations and circumstances but not be blind or pretend
- Accept other people's free will unless clash with self-benefits/well being
- Focus more on what's good, right and positive about others than what's negative, wrong and bad, but don't be blinded to reality.

Lessons about fate:

- Fate seems to be a Catchall term to describe outcomes that are not expected and occur despite apparent self-directive actions.

- Oftentimes, repeated negative consequences has more to do with ones habits, environment, poor coping skills, social situations, social contacts and external competitive forces that repeated seem to thwart one's efforts to succeed at particular pursuits to the level of expected satisfaction.
- Fate is often the juxtaposition of random chance occurrences of events that impact the course of people's lives in unexpected and unexplained ways – whether positive or negative.
- Fate likely does not exist as an intentional operative force in nature, beyond its cyclical, regular patterns and unexpected changes.

Lessons about chance:

- Random chance is no more and no less than probability permutation – the odds of any event happening increases as the activities likely to make an outcome occur increases.
- Good luck or bad luck has more to do with random chance as it is expressed in apparent cycles of ebb and flow.

- On the permutation distribution bell curve, there are those in the extreme of the curve that appear to be more often benefited or hurt by natural and life events beyond one's circumstances.

Lessons about uncertainty:

- The future is unknown.
- Current trends often point to a probable future as it often limits the options that would otherwise remain viable in a course of actions leading to certain consequences.
- Uncertainties are part of reality and life – there is no way to eliminate it from life as events, people, circumstances and situations are dynamic and constantly in a state of flux.
- The most efficient way to deal with uncertainties is to prepare for the worse case scenarios with adequate skills and resources – but also having scaled back subsistent programs in the event ones best laid plans and preparations become inadequate due to the underestimation of the effects and consequential outcomes of uncertainty.

- Living in the present, without future expectations is one way to accept uncertainty – that is to make step by step decision-making as events occur to seek the best path through obstacles.
- Analyzing potential trends and subsequent events, but living in the present by being sensitive to ones immediate environment is a reasonable strategy to deal with uncertainty to minimize anxieties and fears.

Lessons about the world:

- The financial elites have insatiable greed for money and power and don't care at what expense it takes including grave negative consequences to people, nations, governments and the environment.
- Several secretive groups (Globalist bankers, Illuminati, Bildeberg, Masons, Freemasons, etc.) compete for control of the world economy, governments and world resources.
- Everything having to do with high finance and wealth doesn't happen by accident, except for unintended consequences – all involve conspiracies on the highest levels within/between corporations and within/between government agencies/politicians

- Certain industries drive public policy due to political contributions and lobbyists who corrupt public officials and politicians. Among these are insurance companies, pharmaceuticals, investment bankers, commodities exchange and stock market brokers, organized crime syndicates, and labor unions.
- New industries are created often by fake science such as global warming, lead poisoning and asbestos where statistical facts do not support the conclusions. People and businesses that benefit from the hype pressure vote whoring politicians to pass restrictive laws to enhance their profit potential. Others greatly exaggerate the frequency of occurrence by redefining standards to be more inclusive of symptoms that were not descriptive of various syndromes such as autism.
- Certain industries block real scientific facts when it cast negative data on their products – such as cell phone microwave radiation and its long term effect on causing brain lesions and autism in fetus and young children.
- The elite Globalists – particularly the Rothschilds have created and financed wars all over the world for the past 200 years in pursuing their secret greedy plot for global financial domination and control of nations, the global economic system and world resources.

- The elites and powerful generally can skirt the laws applying to the populace due to their ability to manipulate the legal system – unless the crimes are notorious and not adequately planned out by conspirators (such as the JFK assassination and 911).
- The peoples of the world are basically stupid followers who have been socialized to blindly accept social norms, morals and laws without question and to believe in their spirituality and patriotic jingoism even when being manipulated by demigods.
- The vast preponderance of people are fake, expressing selfish desires disguised as altruism, kindness, niceness and politically correct speech – while all along their hidden personal agenda is to obtain the trust of others who they plan to exploit later.
- The Globalist World Order is the perpetual goal of the elite Globalist conspiracy of the Learned Elders of Zion who control Britain and America and have strong inroads to almost all of the major economies of the world – Russia, China, Germany, and many others.
- Given the opportunity, the vast majority of people are corruptible – name the price.
- People can't handle the truth about themselves if it is not complimentary and will become your enemy for bringing it up where an observation becomes criticism.

What gives me joy:

- Seeing bunnies love and groom each other
- Seeing bunnies jumping for joy
- Getting bargains on bunny food – veggies, pellets and hay
- Beer buzz (2-5)
- Singing while buzzed
- Chatting with friends while buzzed
- Good movies
- Good TV show
- Hanging out with Tony
- Karen emails and texts
- Writing
- Good martial arts DVDs

Avoiding unhappiness:

- Unfulfilled expectations
- Betrayal by close friend or relative
- Predatory ingratitude
- Deception and untruthfulness with intent to manipulate
- Getting ripped off
- Feeling physically drained
- Feeling emotionally drained and depressed
- Worried about bunnies health and happiness

- *What makes me miserable:*

- rabbits fighting and bullying
- rabbits sick and suffering
- rabbits dying
- Suzy rants and yelling insults
- Suzy's evil perspectives
- Suzy's selfishness
- Suzy's delusional personality
- mom's stupidity
- illness that makes me tired
- fatigue
- lack of sleep

Lessons about people and social relationships:

- Over 90% of relationships are predatory in nature because people are insecure, inadequate, and selfish.
- People use others to help them to fulfill their personal wants and needs.
- Most people are too burdened with trivial aspects of their lives, socially conditioned norms, and the need for validation from others to actually live lives where they

are actually being their real selves – except in societies where honesty, self expression and forgiveness are social norms.

- A self-actualized person has little need for binding relationships beyond occasional companionship or social conversation.
- People are either generally either exploiters or exploited.
- There are 5 basic types of people

1. *self-actualized – see inner and outer reality for what it is and deals with it*

2. *deniers – refuses to see truth and reality that contradicts or challenges their insular, self-deceptive and delusional perceptions and perspectives.*

3. *wannabees – not satisfied with who they are and their reality and seeks to change mostly according to external models and social norms and values*

4. *self-loathing – despises certain aspects of who they are but disguises it by attacking others with those traits they hate in themselves.*

5. *zombies – don't know who they are, just exist like animals responding to stimuli*

6. *examples of self-actualized is Martin Luther King and Senator Kerri, wannabe is Paris Hilton and self-loathing is Adolf Hitler (globalist bastard).*

- Social conformity, comparison, and cultural tradition causes people to be insecure, judgmental and unhappy – even to do evil inhumane torturous emotional and physical things to other... the emphasis on superiority, winning and wealth.

- *classism – there are superior classes of people with greater value and worth, more deserving to live and control the values in society and people's lives*

- *sexism – men are superior to women due to greater strength and violence*

- *racism – whites and lighter skin people in almost all cultures are superior to the dark skinned people... also dark skin denotes toiling in the sun in most cultures (except whites want a tan to denote leisurely play and rest from resort swimming pools and beaches)- thus denotes a lower class of inferior people*

- *ageism – western society emphasizes youth as being virile, fit, attractive and sexual (commercially exploitable) thus old people are discounted and devalued*

- *intellectualism – degrees and elite institutions and high GPA and standardized test scores increase the social value of people and those with less intellectual capacity and performance are demeaned*

- *wealth – those who accrue more and hoard fortune in excess are admired and described as being successful – a measure that is often perverted in that the methods by which a person acquires wealth is usually not a litmus test of legitimacy or personal humanistic value*
- *fame – social and cultural imperatives that are the consequences of family dynamics, mass media and the education system places undue standards and benchmarks against which people become both internally and externally validated… without which too many people feel inadequate, incomplete, and not valued more in society.*
- *full potential is a paradigm that teachers, parents, and society plays to motivate children and adults to do their best according to their personal potential – however this mantra has become an additional cause of emotional stress, physical injuries, and mental disruption leading to depression and unhappiness due to the extreme difficulty in reaching this elusive full potential goal.*
- *having fun is often given as the reason people do things – however, many of life's responsibilities are difficult, monotonous and sacrifices one's personal benefits to help others.*

What rabbits taught me:

Emotional:

Communicating and interacting with rabbits is primarily emotionally based as they rarely vocalize as dogs or even Cats. Consequently, understanding their needs, feelings and desires depend largely on reading their body language, physical cues, cooperativeness, eating habits, and show of affection. Rabbits are able to communicate with each other and older rabbits teach younger rabbits on certain behaviors, for example:

- Kimberly/Katie told surviving babies to hide in dark corner of compound after sibling was killed by large black cat
- Amberly teaches toddlers to bite through cardboard barriers separating rooms
- Amberly teaches toddlers to poop and pee all over as a way to mark territory
- Amberly refuses to let me pet her after she was moved from living room
- Amberly flung pee on me many times when I wanted her to stay in den previously occupied by Gorby who left his scent everywhere – Amberly hates Gorby and climbed sofa to look out the window to find him.

Relating to rabbits on a personal emotional level instead of a verbal intellectual level made me highly vulnerable to empathetic uncertainties and honest reflection of my heartfelt feelings for another life. Their total dependence on my actions for their lives – their physical and emotional well being is a real and significant responsibility with burdens almost similar to that of raising human children. Particularly with rabbits that I had cared for in excess of 6 months to almost 2 years, my sacrifices, hard work, worries, and affections engendered a sense of duty, obligation and protectionism. In order to replenish their fresh food, pellets and water on a daily basis, twice for pregnant rabbits or moms with kids… and make occasional repairs and/or separate them for fighting after they dug holes into each other's areas, I had to commit myself to a 3-4 hour daily routine to beat sunset – depending on the number of rabbits spread out over the number of living areas. At the maximum there were 70 rabbits and bunnies total (30 new borns) that I cared for spread out over 14 living areas. After the killer Cat ate 8, we sold 9, with 13 new bunnies there was still 18 to care for living in 9 separate living areas, not cages but fenced areas and sections and indoor rooms.

My natural concern was comprehensive, looking after the physical health, comforts, emotional state, activities and interaction relations with other rabbits and with me. Spread out over 35 rabbits was a challenge – even two dozen rabbits involved at least 3 and half hours of work each day. With 18 rabbits and bunnies, the feeding schedule is more manageable – around 2 and half hours daily. I try to spend some time petting and interacting with individual rabbits, but it is unfulfilling because insufficient quality time is spent to engender trust and they tend to run when I try to pet or pick them up. I feel a sense of guilt that while I care sufficiently for their physical needs, I'm not able to spend sufficient time to share and care for their emotional need for attention, grooming and interaction. Consequently, the males constantly want to dig into each others space to fight and more than one nose has been bitten off when they stick their head through the fence into each other's areas.

When I gave away or sold my rabbits or bunnies, I felt saddened and there is an empty feeling in the pit of my solar plexus because I worry about the uncertainty whether they will find a good home, or if they will become abused, tortured, starved, neglected or killed by their new owners, Cats or dogs. It is a psychic burden that stays with me that is difficult to shed... like wondering how human children are taken care when at baby sitters. I hope for the best and feel good when I think someone who Suzy knows will give them a good home with lots of love. I feel badly that I'm not able to spend quality time with the rabbits as I would like – working on their rabbitat and caring for their physical needs averaged 6.6 hours during September just for the outside rabbits – a full time job already. When factoring in the 1-2 hours I spend caring for the indoor rabbits, it was obvious that rabbit care had become a full time responsibility. I worry about my rabbits, if they are content, too hot or too cold, hungry, upset, unhappy or ill. I feel as if they are children who are defenseless and totally rely on me for their every need. It's a responsibility I take seriously and try my best to be reliable, consistent, patient and doing as the labor of love without complaints or regrets.

When Amberly was unhappy we moved her out of the living room after she lived their all year, and spent so much time pooping and peeing in the kitchen, she refused to let me pet her and she flung pee on me half dozen times, including on my face and bed. I felt badly and saddened that our closeness had been wiped out in a day. I felt compassion and understanding that her whole world was turned upside down. I was patient and cleaned the carpet in the den to remove some of Gorby's scent, then brought in carpeting with Amberly's and babies scent along with their feeding dishes. They finally felt at home and enjoyed exploring the den and then huddling together when resting.

The lessons I'm learning about my emotions is to allow myself to feel them fully instead of suppressing them, but rather to be honest with myself and confident in my emotional stability and strength to enable me to feel both the bad with the good and know that I'll be okay and get through it. I feel various intensities of sadness, guilt, and anger when my rabbits die for various reasons – some caused by my stupidity, ignorance, negligence and others by nature or other people. I have to learn to feel and then to get over it and to move on, accepting the outcomes as irreversible and thus not subject to change through agonizing guilt and regret. I am feeling more empathetic to what rabbit might be feeling and thinking as I reflect on how I might feel under similar circumstances.

Consequently, I feel much sadness from time to time, but feel elated when the rabbits and particularly the bunnies are literally jumping for joy. It's almost getting to the point where my life revolves around caring for my rabbits in both their emotional and physical health. I know I need to keep perspective that after all, they are just rabbits and not really human, but the distinction is blurred as I become engrossed in my daily activities and responsibilities to provide the best living conditions I can under my limited and restricted financial and physical situation. Still, I try to learn from my mistakes to do better.

My New World View:

As my rabbits and I communicate only on an emotional level supplemented by body language and cues, the experience has shown me how mammals other than humans exhibit such emotional similarities to that typically expressed by people. Being non-predatory creatures, I only observe their interactions based on personalities that are based primarily on dominance, respect, caring, loyalty and territoriality. They are not capable of killing due to their possession of only 2 top and bottom teeth – as compared to the sharp teeth of predators like Cats and dogs. Consequently, their personalities and character depict interactions that may exemplify those day to day feelings people possess in the course of getting through their days, without deliberate mal intent, but with occasional personality conflicts due primarily to territoriality.

Extrapolating to feelings typically expressed or verbalized by humans, I find distinctly similar qualities, texture, motivations, and expression of emotions by rabbits that are typically exhibited by humans. While humans are generally deceptive and are able to disguise their true feelings, rabbits express what they feel at the moment they feel it and thus are totally honest. If they like you, they let you know by licking you. If they are angry at you, they let you know by flinging urine on you, or running away when you want to pet them. If they are afraid, they hide. When hungry, they flip over their feeding trays or if they don't like what's in the tray. When terrorized by cats, they try to hide their eyes so as not to see it, but they fear imminent death – but can't do much about it except hope the cat can't break into their fenced areas. When in danger, they will thump and when confronted by predators, will flee as fast as possible when chased. Humans respond in similar manners when faced with danger – flight or fight... and it's not uncommon over the history of mankind for entire peoples who succumbed to the brutality of conquering armies – where they are too afraid or weak to fight a superior predator, and too slow to flee its far-reaching strength. The weak simply succumb to the strong. That seems to be the universal constant in nature – weak forces surrendering and becoming dominated or absorbed by the strong.

When we go against the natural order in life, we place ourselves into antagonistic positions to satisfy our ego needs to feel important, self-directed, valuable and validated by others in society. We are encouraged to compare ourselves and our accomplishments to others to justify our stature and value to society. We end up chasing unreasonable dreams at great expenditure of time and effort, not because we really wanted to, but because we've become convinced that's what we're supposed to do. Hope comes from happiness, which is the best shield against depression and despair. If we listen to our hearts and do things that make us happy for ourselves, and not for approval from others, we're likely not depressed.

www.ingramcontent.com/pod-product-compliance
Lightning Source LLC
Chambersburg PA
CBHW070916290526
45795CB00001B/334